SO WORTH IT!

The Guidebook to Success (and Failure) as an Entrepreneur

ISBN 979-8-990-55629-4

Published in Phoenix, Arizona by Emissary Publishing.
Emissary is a business trade name of Ed's Voices, LTD.

The views expressed by the author are those of the author and do not necessarily reflect the views of the publisher

Photography by: The Malicote's Photography

Dedication

To all of those who believed I could,
even when they had no idea what the hell I was doing.

Especially my Mother, Kinch, who was my biggest cheerleader.

TABLE OF CONTENTS

ACKNOWLEDGEMENTS

FOREWORD

INTRODUCTION... 1

PART ONE : INCEPTION

PART THREE : INITIATIVE

PART TWO : INVESTMENT

PART FOUR : INNOVATION

CONCLUSION... 141

NOTES & JOURNALING

W riting this guide was more cathartic than I expected. The original intent was just to get thoughts out of my head; to vent… to myself.

This is a collection of very real failures from ~~15~~ ~~18~~ 20 plus years of management and business ownership, written over a period of ~~3~~ ~~5~~ ~~7~~ 11 years. They were some of the hardest years of my life, professionally and personally. You should know, there were a lot of edits; I like to curse—a lot. And some things happened along the way, about which I added some chapters and notes.

Every time I thought I'd finished, I came back with more content and another round of edits. Throughout the process, I saw my highest highs and lowest lows. Some days I had six figures in the bank and sat atop the world; others I spent broke, desolate, and on the verge of bankruptcy. You will see these notes along the way; I aim to be as genuine as I can be about the good and the bad of entrepreneurship.

I want to thank several people for helping me along the way. Of everyone, my parents deserve the most thanks. They've helped me move, taken me in, and worked events when staff bailed at the last minute. They listened to all my stupid ideas, and helped me get out of most of them (*usually after telling me repeatedly, in advance, not to do them*). They are the most constant sources of love and support, in everything I've done. Dad, you always told me these experiences would eventually give me something to laugh at… Don't let this go to your head.

My mother is amazing and helped me get my business started. She worked with me in a number of ways until her sudden death in 2023.

And to my wife, Molly, who now takes the role my parents once had of working events, listening to my "next big thing," working around my crazy schedule, and being the ultimate hype woman.

Over the last decade, I've been privileged to stand shoulder-to-shoulder with the woman who wrote this book. We've laughed through chaos, cheered each other on through business launches and big leaps, cried through tough seasons of life and leadership, and most meaningfully—we've grown up together as women, mothers, and entrepreneurs. This book, *So Worth It*, is a reflection of every ounce of grit, heart, and hard-won wisdom Kaelyn has earned—and she now hands it to you – no filter, no fluff.

We first met while building businesses and trying to figure out how to juggle ambition with real life. We didn't have it all mapped out (who does?), but we had drive, vision, and a mutual respect for the hustle it takes to do things your own way. Over the years, Kaelyn became one of the few people I could call when I needed real-talk advice—someone who understood that running a business isn't just strategy and spreadsheets. It's deeply personal; you navigate late nights and tight budgets, balance motherhood and meetings, swallow your pride and pitch anyway, learn the hard way (and then learn it again), and wake up the next day still chasing the dream.

This book is like having that kind of friend in your back pocket.

What I love most about *So Worth It* is that Kaelyn never romanticizes the entrepreneurial journey.

She's not trying to sell you on a highlight reel. Instead, she walks you through the mess and magic of building something from the ground up. Chapter by chapter, you'll find equal parts permission and push: permission to not have it all figured out yet—and a push to keep moving forward anyway.

From developing your idea, to navigating clients, finances, growth, and media, to the less glamorous stuff like taxes, trademarks, and the dreaded white noise of bad advice and burnout—this book holds nothing back. It's tactical, honest, funny, and most of all, *real*. You'll recognize your own fears and dreams in these pages. You'll find stories that make you laugh out loud and others that hit a little too close to home. That's the point. This isn't a business textbook—it's a manual for the brave.

And it *is* brave to start something. To bet on yourself. To choose a path that isn't always clear, supported, or celebrated. It's brave to say, "I believe in this enough to risk failing for it." And it's even braver to keep going when it gets hard.

Kaelyn knows hard. She's walked through uncertainty, criticism, and reinvention. She's built and rebuilt. She's done the lonely work of trusting herself when no one else had the full picture. And she's still standing—not just standing, but thriving and lifting others up along the way.

This isn't just a how-to book. It's a "you're not alone" book. It says: I've been there. I've made the mistakes. I've learned what works—and what doesn't. I've sat in the quiet and wondered if it's all worth it. And I'm here to tell you: *It is.*

Whether you're just beginning or deep in the game, this book will meet you where you are. It will challenge, encourage, and equip you. And if you let it, it will remind you that your voice, vision, and work matter.

The truth is, no one's coming to give you permission. You won't ever feel fully ready. But you *are* capable. And the fact that you're holding this book in your hands tells me you're already in the arena.

So take a deep breath. Get honest with yourself. Write in the margins. Ask the hard questions. Celebrate the wins, grieve the losses, and keep going.

You're not alone—and you're not crazy.
You're just brave enough to believe that your dream is so worth it.

Because it is. And so are you.
Keep shining your light,

Vitale Buford Hardin
CEO, Vitale & Company

INTRODUCTION

Chapter Extras

Let me guess…

You have the next BIG THING. You want to be your own boss, and you want the time, freedom, and flexibility that comes with owning a company. And who doesn't want to decide their own salary, right?!

Maybe I'm the first to tell you, but starting a business also sucks. It brings difficulty, frustration, tons of work and stress, and requires a ton of time and patience. It's hard… but it's so worth it.

I started my first business in high school, though I didn't yet realize it. To be honest, it wasn't so much a business as it was a passion or hobby. Ten years later, it became a real business. I spent that decade building, growing, and slowly creating it. Then, the restaurant I managed at the time announced their closing, so I decided to take the leap into full-time entrepreneurship.

I am very "Type A." I don't mind taking risks, but I prefer them when paired with a good plan. I have my whole life planned out, and I don't take a single step before thinking through the following two. My father would disagree and tell you I'm impulsive and impatient. I like to think I'm passionate and determined. I never thought I would get to where I am today. If you'd told me ten years ago what today would look like, I'd have laughed at you. If you'd told me in 2013 how my company would grow, and also disappear, and that I would rework my personal journal into a published book, I'd have laughed even more. If anyone had told me how much effort starting a business would take, I don't know if I would have done it. But I'm glad I did.

To this day, I'm not sure how I figured out how to make it all work. After more than twenty years from hobby to thriving business, I still feel like I have very little truly "figured out." I'm still learning and adjusting along the way. But had there been a 'how-to guide' on starting a business, with stories about its difficulties and the obstacles you have to overcome, I would have thought long and hard about owning a small business. Few other efforts have taken so much out of me, and I don't recommend it for everyone.

Starting a business takes guts, risks, inspiration, motivation, time, money, energy, emotions, organization, time, money… and so much more. You must become your own toughest challenger—as well as your own biggest cheerleader. Stay highly organized, and force yourself to work harder and longer every day. You must become the most determined optimist in the room, even when it feels like everything's crashing down around you. You must be strong and passionate. Starting a business, no matter its size or type, takes everything you have—and then some. Success comes from hard work + risk + late nights + struggles + failures + persistence + discipline + exhaustion + doubts + 'code blues' + criticism + disappointments + sleep deprivation + rejections + sacrifices + tears + passion + heart.

Why read this book?

I based this book on my experience starting and running small businesses. It shows the dirty, messy, beautiful truth about getting started. I wanted to give you an honest look at the best and worst parts about owning a small business—and the stories, tips, and advice I found helpful along the way. If you seriously want to consider starting a business, these are twelve areas you should think about before you jump in the pool, to avoid drowning.

These rules aren't the ONLY things to consider. Most start-ups fail within the first year—and the ones that survive fail within years three to five. If you can make it to year five, you're onto something. Sometimes, even if you make it to year five, you get blindsided in year seven and have to fold, despite your most intense efforts and best of intentions. But no matter how far you get, at least you can say you had the passion and guts to try. The purpose of this guide is to share advice about the trials and tribulations I faced starting my own company… including the many mistakes I made. It may deter you from starting something you'd regret, or perhaps it will spark more passion and determination for you to push forward.

My dad always told me, "The best way to learn is to hit every pothole on the drive—just make sure you hit each pothole only once." While there are potholes you MUST hit to learn the ins and outs of running your business, there are other potholes that are avoidable if you see them coming. I'm handing you the roadmap for the potholes I hit unnecessarily, so you can dodge them on your business ownership journey.

Use this book as a guide. Take notes, write down thoughts, highlight like crazy, and use it as a working manual for your business. Work through the first six chapters, implement them, then come back and work through the last six. And then, start again. Focus on your business for a year and then revisit the guide from the beginning. Better yet – buy a few extra copies, and compare how you fill it out each year.

I've included activities and questions to get you thinking critically, as well as several motivational and inspirational quotes mixed with words of wisdom you should take seriously. Additionally, by scanning the QR codes you see throughout the book, you'll find more content, exercises, and real-life stories from other small business owners on my website. Buckle up!

First, take this quick test. ⟶ Circle the items below that matter to you the most.

And before we get started, I need you to read this out loud (yes, really):

I am worth it. I matter.
I can do anything I want if I work hard and put my mind to it.
I am smart. I am going to make a difference.
I can do this.

Why say this out loud? Because you're going to need to say it. A lot. You're going to feel torn down, defeated, exhausted, and everything in between—and you need to repeat this often to keep your eye on the prize. No one will hand success to you on a silver platter. You will have to work for it, fight for it, and in some cases you'll have to take it—forcefully.

Kaelyn Query.

Choose the ones you would <u>refuse</u> to give up to start your small business.

Total your score, one point for each item. We will revisit this later at the end of the manual.

10 Family

9 Friends

8 Money

7 Nights and weekends off

6 House, car, other property

5 Vacations

4 Steady pay checks

3 Events with your friends

2 Freedom

1 Making your own schedule

Total Score: _____

INCEPTION:
YOU HAVE AN IDEA

01 | MAP IT OUT
DO SOME RESEARCH
PASSION
MENTORS & ADVISORS
NETWORKING

Chapter Extras

When I started my first official company, LexEffect Events, I meant for it to become a non-profit foundation. I wanted to host fundraising events and raise money for other non-profit organizations. We would then use the proceeds to offer grants to other non-profits, to support their individual missions.

Sounds like a great idea, right?

Wrong! It was a terrible idea. As I thought it through, I realized I wanted to host several events that non-profit organizations could not support. Either the events had formats that clashed with non-profit rules, or the type of company we needed to build was itself at odds with non-profit structure requirements. If you've ever looked at the paperwork and rules to become a 501©*anything*, you know—they're insane.

I don't like rules. Non-profits have *so* many rules. So I threw that idea out the window, and I reworked the purpose of LexEffect Events.

Map It Out

You have an idea. Maybe it's the beginnings of the next billion-dollar company, product, service, or [insert brilliant idea here]… right? Of course. While you might be onto something, remember: Every day, thousands of people come up with their own ideas for the "next big thing." If you want to take yours seriously, it's time to understand how to take it from an idea to a reality.

Do you have a product, or a service?
Can you explain the benefits?
What does it look like to you?
What would it look like for your customer?

You need to write down the real details about this idea, and then let it sit. Think about it, come back, and edit it again. And then, do it again. If you can't clearly articulate your idea, you won't get very far.

Try answering these questions:

What is it?
How does it work? Who is it for?
Who does it benefit?
Why am I doing it?
What problem does it solve?
How does it make money?

Once you put your thoughts on paper, it'll force you to tweak your vision, especially when you let other people examine it. Hell, you may even change your vision altogether. And that's okay—even expected.

The process of fleshing out an idea is to explore the concept from multiple angles.

Is someone else already offering this product or service?

If yes, is their business successful?

Is there still a market for you to launch something similar?

What do you bring to the table that the current company doesn't?

On the other hand .. if *nobody* offers this product or service - why not? Did someone try and quit because of regulations, licensing, expenses, or some other reason? These are important to answer before investing time, energy, or money in your new venture.

When I put pen to paper, my ideas get one step closer to becoming realities. I keep a journal with me everywhere I go, and write down quotes, company names, URL ideas, business ideas, and concepts. Anything that comes to mind goes in my book. Most of it never makes it past the paper; I either get bored with an idea, or it stops making sense, so I leave it.

But sometimes, when time slows down and creative juices flow, ideas grow legs. I start mapping out ideas that feel like they could go somewhere, and the more I think about them, the better they become. Sometimes, the ideas become business plans; I draft an outline on the computer, and soon I have a solid plan with projections and a logo. Every so often, one of them goes all the way, and I launch a grand opening.

One year, after several successful venue management ventures, I got the opportunity to open my own venue. I had no partners or help —just me. At first, I said "No." It was a *huge* commitment, and I wasn't sure I wanted the risk. I'd recently split with another venue partnership where I'd lost money.

But the idea stuck with me, so I went home and took time to map out the business. How would it work? How would it run? What would I do if I didn't have someone else telling me how to run the operations and I could make those calls for myself?

Then, I crunched the numbers. Based on the size of the space, I calculated what would I charge customers to use it. I thought through who I would serve as my target audience. I dreamed of the kind of company I'd build If I got to make all the decisions.

The numbers worked, and I felt more confident. I called back and said I'd take the space. We launched "Limestone Hall" in 2017, and officially opened our doors in February of 2018. When we opened, I had over a year's worth of revenue in the bank. We never had to worry about finances for a single day—not even during COVID. I sold that venue in December of 2022, and it remains a popular event space in Lexington to this day.

Explore Your Idea

More online:

Do Some Research

Prior to this, I launched the Moontower Music Festival in Midway, Kentucky. In its first year, about six bands performed onstage in a vineyard at this small, one-day festival. I funded it with my own money, plus ticket sales and a handful of sponsors. The bands were alternative, rock, and jam bands. About eight hundred people showed up.

It was awesome.

Our team was eager to produce the festival. I had experience working with much larger music festivals, so I felt like we could give it a good run. But we needed to know if it would work in our area before we threw money at it. Was there a market for another music festival in the region? Several larger music festivals took place just an hour from Midway in Louisville and Cincinnati. Did Lexington have enough people interested in this kind of music so we could pull it off? If we started small, could we eventually grow it into a bigger festival like Forecastle or Bonnaroo?

We researched extensively. We put out surveys, dug into data from those two major festivals, and studied the radius clauses of other nearby festivals to see which dates would work (and allow us to avoid getting drowned out by larger events). We shared our ideas with the tourism department, local hotels, and the Chamber of Commerce. Finally, we had enough data to make an informed decision—and it worked. We knew a market existed for the festival. We knew Lexington wanted something like this—and almost 1,000 people showed up the first year to prove it. We produced a few stand-alone concerts and shows in advance to test the genre in this market, which traditionally skewed toward country music. They sold out (with a wait list) and people begged for more. We knew we needed to scale slowly to make it grow—but we felt confident it would work.

That's how you pursue an idea. You start with research. For the music festival, we considered:

- **Who else produced a similar music festival in the city?** *At the time, a very popular country music festival happened around the Fourth of July, and others put on smaller festivals in nearby cities throughout the year. Additionally, several larger multi-day* *festivals took place in Louisville and Cincinnati, both about an hour away from Lexington.*

- **Did people want or need it?** *With our surveys and focus groups, we discovered a group of people who wanted to attend concerts like ours. We extended that research to smaller, single shows, and when we found traction with them, we knew we stood on solid ground.*

- **Could we start small and then scale?** *With this festival, we could. We had smaller outdoor venues that worked well for the same type of event. We had great community partners who would jump in for sponsorships and support. And we had the capital to fund a small, initial version of the festival.*

As you map out your idea, consider these questions:

1. Who already provides your product/service?

2. Are/were they successful in doing so?

   1. If yes, can you find a market or niche to offer a similar product or service?

   2. If not, how can you tweak or adjust to make up for their problems?

2. If they weren't successful, why?
   Sometimes, you can see an opportunity to trailblaze in an underserved area. But it could also mean that you don't have a realistic idea. Someone once pitched to me about creating a company to produce a unique, personalized wedding gift. They wanted to create an exciting memento for couples to keep from their special day. They did it for their own wedding and thought they could turn it into a business. While it was a nice idea in theory, the high cost of producing their product left no margin for profit. A profit margin of zero defeats the purpose of starting a business.

3. Do you need any special classifications, degrees, or certifications?

4. Can you realistically start this venture on the side, or do you have to jump into a full-time effort from the start?

During your research, create a SWOT analysis of your product or service. Name the **S**trengths and **W**eaknesses of your service or brand. Identify the **O**pportunities to grow, sell, or expand, and take inventory of the **T**hreats that could prevent your idea from coming to life.

Strengths: Qualities that separate you from a potential competitor, such as internal resources, potential assets, prior experience.

Weaknesses: Things and attributes competitors have, which your company lacks. Your natural limitations and areas of incompetence.

Opportunities: Underserved markets where there is demand for your product/service. The people most likely to buy what you offer are usually the ones most starved for its benefits.

Threats: Competitors. Laws and regulations. Certifications or degrees. Pre-existing negative feelings from the public towards your product/service. All of these could stifle your success.

Consider Apple as an example. When they launched the Apple-1 (first personal computer) in 1976, they probably assumed their strength lay in entering a blue ocean market as one of the first companies to produce a computer like this. They built the computer to allow an individual house or small company the ability to do the same work as a large corporation.

Apple's weaknesses were that very few people owned personal computers, and most couldn't afford it. They had to find a way to produce an affordable computer AND explain to people why they should want one for their home. Another weakness was that nobody knew who they were. Unlike today, where we know Apple's every move within minutes, they didn't have any brand recognition.

Now fast forward and look at Apple's SWOT in 2025: a stable company, known for innovative technology, with high value brand reputation and a long track record of

Ideas:

use this space to brainstorm your business ideas

success. Apple can sell phones for upwards of one thousand dollars, and no one bats an eye. People line up outside Apple's retail locations every time the company releases a new iPhone.

Domino's, founded in 1960 in Ann Arbor, Michigan, is the second largest pizza delivery chain in the world, and promotes "consistent delivery of quality pizza." They lean on their strengths of brand recognition and affordability to help drive profits, and with technology innovation they are able to track deliveries and improve systems with each store. After a string of bad deliveries across the company, they turned their weakness into an opportunity to re-engage customers for a second chance. This was the source of their "30-minute promise," for which they became a household name. Today, Domino's lives in a saturated market. When they launched, there were far fewer pizza chains or delivery services like GrubHub and DoorDash.

We launched a series of farm-to table dinner events called "Chew," held quarterly in its first year. We began with the theme "Four Seasons." Each chef had to create a three-course dinner using local ingredients, inspired by the season they picked. Each dinner was held in a different, non-traditional venue (gardens, parking lots, galleries, and more), and we paired local beer, wine, and spirits with each course.

Chew was a hit, and we got in early on the farm-to-table trend. We created a unique, interesting, and affordable series of events where the strengths and opportunities outweighed the weaknesses and threats. We needed to make money, of course, so we increased frequency and decreased the price of admission. While similar events took place in nearby cities, they only happened

SWOT Analysis

More online:

Strengths

Weaknesses

Opportunities

Threats

once or twice a year, themed around larger events (like the Kentucky Derby). Seating was more limited, and tickets more expensive. The market wasn't too saturated and we provided a farm-to-table experience at an approachable, full-service price point. Our opportunity was (eventually) to expand the series, as we worked through the kinks and realized there was a big market for this type of event. Also, we allowed attendees to explore new venues, something no other dinner experience offered.

Our main weakness was low visibility; we were a new company with a small following, so we leaned on grassroots marketing (mostly free social media) and word-of-mouth to attract customers. We faced the threat that others would launch similar dinner series or events, saturating the market and making it harder to sell our tickets. Restaurants, for example, that already had the venue, staff, equipment, and customer base, could enter the market easily, smoothly and at a lower price point.

By running the SWOT questions and following the analysis, we grew the Chew series to feature six dinners and a slew of brunch events, too. The SWOT served as a roadmap for our planning and helped us identify hazards to avoid or overcome.

So let's map it out. Scan the QR code for a downloadable worksheet to work through the sections we've just covered.

Passion

I'm passionate about travel. I think it ties into my love of cooking and entertaining; there's something about traveling somewhere I've never seen and exploring the culture through food, music, and history. In 2019, I traveled through Spain, France, Monaco, and Italy by myself for about three and a half weeks. I get excited by everything I get to see and do and about the possibilities of exploring new places. It doesn't matter if I get a one-day trip or a month-long adventure, travel refills my cup. I come home energized. When I feel like I'm in a rut, I look at my calendar to check the last time I took a trip. If you ask me about a trip I've recently taken or a trip coming up, you'll see a light in my eye and excitement in my voice.

Now that you've spent time mapping out and researching your idea and you're ready to move forward and turn this into a business, ask yourself: "Am I really passionate about this business?"

So...
Are you *really* passionate about it?

It's a good idea to know where you *lack* passion—so you can make an informed commitment you're likely to keep. Some activities and obstacles can be completely avoided in business (I do event planning, but not crane operation), while others (like accounting and digital marketing) are part of the gig. If you know what you're **not** passionate about, you have a better idea of areas to minimize or avoid completely. You can identify where you'll struggle and need someone else to do the heavy lifting.

Will you live, eat, breathe, sleep, and bleed for this dream? Will you give up friends, family, money, sanity, opportunities, relationships, a social life, your house, everything—for it? If the answer is "No," stop reading now and wait for your next big idea.

On the other hand, if you answer "Yes"… you're full of shit. No one *really* believes they'll have to give all of that up. But trust me, you will. You give up some things temporarily, while others are permanent. Right or wrong, sometimes it's the nature of the beast.

Early in my journey, I worked 100-plus-hour weeks. I had zero time for anything other than work. I believed that if I didn't stay busy, I wouldn't be successful. The busier I kept, I assumed, the better my company would perform. I needed to get our name out there and generate cash flow, so I took any and every gig that came my way. I priced things incorrectly, and spread myself thin… and it led to burnout.

I went into the office around 6:00 every morning. I *loved* this time—just me and the kitchen staff at the restaurant across the street. The city was quiet; my mind was calm. I could get more done between 6:00 and 9:00 than most people could in an entire week. I'd work on proposals, invoices, payroll—whatever required concentration and quiet (and math).

Then, from 9:00 to 5:00, I did "business as usual."

From 5:00 until midnight, I'd go to networking events, meet with clients, produce events… and on some occasions, I'd go back to the office and work some more. I thought I was being productive. I thought I was crushing the business ownership "game." I didn't really have a choice—I'd overloaded my schedule so much that it required a ton of work and time to maintain. I couldn't ask the team to do it. That would have been illegal (breaks are required, it turns out), not to mention it would have created a negative work environment. We had too much going on and not enough staff to cover the workload. Because we charged incorrectly, we had too much work and not enough money. I had a hard time letting go of control of all the details, and I struggled to delegate tasks to the team. I always had my hands "in" everything.

Fast-forward several years. I was *done* with events, running my company, being in charge, and working all those hours. I missed *so* many things—celebrations, bachelorette trips, games, birthdays, and holidays. I couldn't tell you what a weekend looked like, and I hadn't had a true vacation (where you totally "check out") since high school. I decided to sell one company, close another, and go back to work for someone else.

The job I found lasted five months, until I couldn't handle it any more. I needed the freedom and flexibility of being my own boss. I am the best (and worst) employee a company could hope for. Additionally, the company furloughed the entire team with very little notice… so I didn't really have a choice. That turned out to be a blessing in disguise, and a great opportunity to learn and refocus. During those five months, I revived my passion. It gave me a renewed sense of purpose, vision, and direction. I created a new set of goals and a new vision for my company. For the remaining eleven months of the year, I put my head down and restarted the marketing and networking. By the end of that year, I'd met or exceeded 80% of my goals—including my revenue goal, which I exceeded by 99.7 percent.

Passion ebbs and flows, but it never truly goes away. If you feel the passion burning you up on the inside, to the point you'll go out of your way for long periods of time in pursuing it … you'll go far in business.

Mentors & Advisors

I live in Kentucky. During my initial research phase of building LexEffect, I found a company in Colorado that staged fun-runs and 5ks. I didn't want to produce these types of events, but they would qualify as "competitive" with my company. This company produced them *very* successfully, and far away enough geographically that they wouldn't threaten me. I tracked down the founder's email and reached out, introducing myself as a "gal from Kentucky starting an event management company." I asked if I might pick his brain from time to time. I knew he was busy, so I told him I wouldn't bother him often, only an occasional email with questions with industry-related questions.

To my surprise, he responded and said, "Yes." I have family in Colorado and spend a lot of time there, so I promised to look him up the next time I was in the area. We met for drinks during my next work trip, and I drained him of every carrot he could dish. That conversation, along with some emails and phone calls, was one of the best things I did in the beginning. He helped me evaluate my plans and goals. Plus, he gave great advice on a few things *not* to do based on his own collection of early mistakes.

The best way you can help yourself in the early stages of business is to build a "brain trust"—a team of advisors and mentors to guide you along the way. Find people who excel in areas you suck at, as well as leaders and trailblazers in your industry. They can help you steer clear of landmines they learned about the hard way. As John Maxwell says, "A leader is a person who knows the way, goes the way, and shows the way."

More online:

When looking for advisors and mentors, keep a few important characteristics in mind:

1) Research people you want to learn from. Do you know their background and expertise? Do they have a connection to what you do? How can they help you, and how can you help them? Do you see any conflicts of interest?

2) Be selective of who you bring into your circle. Choose a few locals who understand your market and area, but don't forget to add outsiders who offer a different perspective.

3) Bring in a variety of industries and professionals. Find a CPA, a marketing pro, an attorney, someone big with the City or the Chamber, someone in a successful non-profit, and so forth. Seek out a good mix of men and women, old and young, different ethnicities, and a variety of backgrounds and experience. The mentors you choose may vary based on your industry, product, or service. My mentor, Jason, once said, "Soliciting advice is like a lighthouse to a ship needing direction. Some lighthouses show the way to go, while some are a warning of where *not* to go. Some are both." I love this analogy; a variety of viewpoints will only help the success of your business.

How do you get these people to become mentors? It's simple—just ask.

Keep in mind, however, mentors probably run their own company and have busy schedules. Use their time wisely and sparingly. Make phone calls or meetings worth their time. Gather thoughts and questions in advance, and don't take longer than an hour when you meet with them. Try to limit calls or meetings to once a month.

Even so, it's good to remember that good mentors and advisors enjoy teaching. They like helping others get started and make progress. They remember their own beginnings, and find fulfillment in sharing what they've learned and experienced.

My mentor in Colorado taught me about buying inventory. He described how he purchased a ton of inventory in the early stages of his career. That might not sound bad … but there was more to the story. They had to store, maintain, and insure the inventory as well. They had to set it up and break it down at every event, which cost them a lot of time and money. With the events he created, they had to haul that inventory all over the country. It wasn't worth the hassle, so eventually he sold the equipment and switched to subleasing.

Knowing this saved me a ton of money, time, and headache. I learned early that I could sublease equipment, bill it to the client, and charge for managing the efforts. If I'd purchased those items instead, I'd have had to deal with the back-end of managing them. Tables, for example, cost $50-$150 apiece, but you have to store them when they're not in use. Tables take up a *lot* of space. When you eventually need them, you also need a vehicle to transport them—and five-foot round tables don't fit in the back of a normal van or SUV! Plus, you need labor to deliver them, set them up, and pick them up. Plus you need insurance in case of damage, and don't forget about general wear-and-tear and eventually replacing them.

All told, the true cost of each table was probably closer to $200-$250 or more, depending on how often we used them. For events with hundreds of people, that meant a lot of tables! It was far better to rent the table for $9, plus sales tax and a minimal delivery fee. That put the rental company in charge of the other overhead expenses, so I could rent the table to the client for $15 and call it a day. Maybe I earned the same gross revenue… but my profit margin was way higher—not to mention what I saved in energy and effort!

I took this a step further and negotiated exclusive agreements with rental companies to prioritize our events over others, and they gave us a reduced rate for exclusivity. This allowed me to make a higher profit on these items, while keeping our output for storage, hauling, and maintaining a large inventory at a bare minimum. It gave us a win-win-win.

I wouldn't have learned that so quickly without my mentor. We continue to track our sales for subleased items and weigh the difference between owning and renting. Based on the number of events we produce each year, we save tens of thousands of dollars in expenses related to rentals, and net $60,000-$80,000 in profit from subrentals.

Networking

Early in my career, I met a guy named Shawn. Shawn is a master of connecting people—not as his job; it's just who he is. Shawn can work a room, he's never met a stranger, and Shawn does something most of us fail doing when networking - he listens more than he talks. We worked in a group together on a networking series called the "Lexington Calendar Project." This monthly event gathered twenty to thirty people, half from private businesses and half from non-profits. We met in a different location each month, and networked around some kind of ice breaker: goldfish races, chicken-shit bingo, badminton, relay races, you name it. It *always* got people talking. It was casual and laid back, and people loved it. None of us got paid to be there; in fact, most of us paid to be a part of it. But it induced the most authentic networking you could find, and I built a few relationships and partnerships that I still call on today. Shawn has always been one of my biggest cheerleaders, and he still recommends me to people and sends referrals our way.

Find your "Shawn"—and *be* a Shawn. I attended events at the Chamber on a regular basis, and I joined every business owner group I could find. I still belong to some of these groups. If you do nothing else, you must become good at networking. I can't overstate the importance of this - it's so important, we've created a list of resources to help you get started using the QR code to the right. You are about to start a business, which means you must become your brand. Whether you're native or new in town, you'll find plenty of people to meet. Join business groups to build your network. I suggest a Young Professionals or small business networking group. The Chamber of Commerce website or your local Visitors Center usually have details on where to find them.

Notes & Journaling:
use this space for notes, thoughts on the first chapter, or a place to jot down ideas

INCEPTION:
GETTING STARTED

02 | **SMALL BUSINESS DEVELOPMENT**
| **MAKE IT OFFICIAL**
| **ELEVATOR PITCH**
| **NETWORKING**

Chapter Extras

You've mapped out your idea, completed your research, and you're ready to move forward. What should you do next? I had no idea where to go, who to ask, or what I needed to start a business. You can try a quick Google search (good luck with that), but you'll get a bunch of insane results. You'll find tons of rules, processes, and information about the dreaded IRS (scary!). Getting your steps right in the beginning will save you money and time later on. Attorneys, CPAs, and other service providers all charge by the hour... so how do you know what you really need for your business?

Small Business Development

You can find hubs around the country through the Small Business Development Centers network. These hubs are a saving grace and the *only* reason I still run a company today. Most towns have SBDCs, and a quick Google search of "Small Business Development Centers" with your city and state will give you a list of them in your area. You must apply and read through their website to ensure you qualify for their services. Personally, I cannot sing their praises enough. Without the help of my advisor, Jay, I wouldn't have the success I do today. These centers provide free or low-cost help for... wait for it... *starting a business*. They give you a checklist of tasks and permits you need to apply for,

but they also provide ongoing guidance and counseling. Take advantage of their offers.

The University of Kentucky's SBDC in Lexington was a free service, and they became my built-in cheerleading squad. Jay wisely told me "No" several times, which helped me avoid numerous bad ideas and saved me a ton of money. Business owners get caught up in ideas easily, and if you think the way I do, every one of them is "great," "perfect," and "bound to be successful." (*Allow me to slap my head as I think back on some of my ideas and shudder*.) Jay helped me weed out bad ideas and define good ones. For years, I received cards from Jay when he saw me in the news, or when I won another award. Long after he left the UKSBDC, he still kept an eye on me and cheered me on.

I also met Sean, the web guy at the UKSBDC. He taught me marketing, websites, and social media. Even today, I can ask him a question, and he will help me. They also had an accountant on hand who would come to my office and look through my QuickBooks accounts. He would tell me where I had screwed up, and then help me fix it. He taught me about payments and clients and lists and categories—and all for free. The entire UKSBDC team (Becky, Fausto, Sherie) cheered me on. They helped spread the word about my business and services, sent me clients and recommendations, submitted my name for awards, and helped me get speaking engagements. I didn't realize it at the time, but they were like a sales team I didn't have to pay for. If that wasn't enough, the UKSBDC hosted countless networking events and seminars or classes where we could learn, meet new people, and continue to grow our business.

Make It Official

You have to fill out about sixty forms to become an official "business." (*Ok, maybe I'm dramatic—there aren't sixty, but it sure felt like it.*) SBDC staff can help you figure out what these forms are, which ones you need, and where to find them. (*The only thing I found scarier than starting a business is buying a house. You fill out one page after another, and you sign your life away to a mortgage company. That shit is scary.*) The SBDC can also help you figure out which type of filing you need to have for taxes – LLC versus S-Corp, for example. But, in case you choose to ignore my advice and just want an easy list, I'll share a few items you need to have in order to make it official:

- Incorporate (LLC, S-Corp, C-Corp, Holdings, etc.)
- Secretary of State form for a tax ID (Also known as an EIN)

- A name for your company (duh …)
- A Sales tax number (depending on the type of business)
- Company Bank Account (no, you may NOT use your personal checking account)
- Website and domain name (see chapter on Media)
- Business cards

It will cost a little to get these things set up, but most of them "pinball" off of one another. If you lack one, you'll be ineligible for another. It's far better to seek the help of the SBDC. Just do it.

Consult with an accountant or CPA as to which type of incorporation you should file. You'll save time and money later on, in the event you decide to change your filing. You could file in two hundred different ways, according to your type of business/product/service, how you conduct business, and a gazillion other factors. Ask an expert; don't try and guess, because this can mean life or death for your business.

Additionally, consider hiring an attorney to help you with this filing. We love to get free help, but depending on your product, service, or business, you may have additional permits you need to apply for, licenses you need to have, or other factors you haven't thought of—and an attorney can help sort through that. You'll have annual filing you must complete with the Secretary of State, and plenty of paperwork, so have an expert help you.

Have you given up yet?
Kudos to you if you're still with me.

Elevator Pitch

My friend, Shawn, taught me about "elevator pitches." Mine sucked. I met Shawn through a mutual friend/client, and we had similar interests. We became friends because we were both crazy and over-committed, and somehow, we found time to stay connected and talk each other through growth as business leaders. When I first met him, he asked the typical, "So, what do you do?" My face lit up. I went into my regular thirty-minute shpiel about LexEffect Events—who we are and what we do, what we plan to do and how cool it is, our clients, and "Oh my gosh, we are so excited, and this is great!" (*In those days, people only asked me that question once… no one made the mistake twice.*)

As I told Shawn my (*obviously*) interesting elevator pitch, I watched his face betray confusion and annoyance. He didn't want a novel-length "pitch"—he just wanted the skinny. About three minutes into my monologue, his eyebrows furrowed. At six-minutes, his eyes glazed over. At the twelve-minute mark, he began looking around the room, trying to lock eyes with anyone who could save him from the conversation. Finally, he stopped me and said, "We need to work on your elevator pitch." It was his polite way of telling me to stop talking.

Your elevator pitch is one of the most important pieces in presenting your brand, especially in the beginning. You have about three seconds to make an impression. Attention spans are short, networking events are awkward, and people get distracted—so if you're going to tell someone what you do, tell them in three seconds.

I felt *pissed* when I learned this. How can you possibly tell someone about all the cool things you're doing in three seconds?! But I promise–you can do it. You simply need to decide what your core functions are. What's the "gist" of what you do? What sets you apart from other people? What is your basic business model? Take a look at the difference in my pitches before and after Shawn:

Original Elevator Pitch:

"I own LexEffect Events and Management. We are a management company that provides free event management services for non-profits, as well as consulting, and we donate money to them from other events we do. We also work on private events like weddings, corporate functions, tradeshows, etc. They pay us a flat fee to plan, promote, and manage their events for them. We also do this for public events, like the

MoonTower Music Festival, The Bourbon Social, CHEW Dinner Series, and more." (*takes breath*)

The first pitch left people confused and overwhelmed. (I talk way too fast, as it is.) It also failed to explain what I did for a living. It took a long time to understand that people didn't care to listen to me ramble for thirty minutes. They may have responded politely, but they preferred a quick answer. If they truly wanted to know more, they would ask.

Your pitch will also change, over time. As your company grows, expands, and changes, so will your pitch. LexEffect started out coordinating events for nonprofits, free of charge. It didn't matter how many non-profits reached out, we worked on their events for free. This was a great way to get our name out there and spread the word. But once our business took off, we didn't have time to give out so much free work. So we limited ourselves to a certain number per year, and only non-profit clients that matched our mission qualified for the free service. Our pitch needed to change because our business had evolved.

Revised Elevator Pitch (after I got my act together):

"LexEffect Events + Management is an event management, planning, and consulting firm based in Kentucky. We produce private and public events across the country, including festivals, trade shows, weddings, social gatherings, fundraisers, and more."

That's it.

It's really true that "less is more." When I gave the short pitch, it allowed people space to ask questions—especially questions relevant to *them*. Sometimes, people's questions lead you to discover who they are, what they do, and which opportunities they might have *for you*. I've generated more new business by keeping my mouth shut after my pitch than any rant I ever gave about the last seventy-two events and how great they all were.

Technology helps with this. In 2013, Facebook was the only social platform that allowed businesses to have a profile. With all the development since then, you don't have to constantly pitch anymore. The internet now does it for you. You can "present" yourself 24 hours a day, without ever speaking to anyone. Whether through a website, a blog, or your social media accounts - you can showcase your style, talents, and expertise to viewers in real-time.

What's *Your* Pitch?

Networking

Now that you've got the ball rolling and you want to tell people about your new company, you need to step up your networking game. Networking is awkward. You have to walk a fine line of talking about yourself—but not too much. Don't miss opportunities to promote your business when the right moment pops up. When I first started, I went to events and tried talking to as many people as possible. I didn't focus on meaningful conversations; I focused on the number of conversations. And I didn't listen to people either; I just went through the motions. I hoped that if I had enough conversations, eventually someone would call me about an event. Once, I paid so little attention while networking that I walked up to the same person *three* times and introduced myself... at the same event. Talk about embarrassing! That guy never called me to produce an event.

If you have the money, I suggest joining your local Chamber of Commerce. Like the SBDC, the Chamber has several avenues that help new businesses. Most are free or very low-cost. Chambers can help promote your product or service, and they have a *ton* of networking opportunities where you can mingle with other business owners. You typically pay an annual fee, which you should add to your budget. Bite the bullet, find the group(s) that work for you, and sign up.

Let me tell you about another reason for joining a Chamber: advocacy work. Chambers work hard on your behalf to advocate for the issues important to their members. So if you feel passionately about city or state laws, taxes, or policies being changed in ways that might benefit or hurt your company, you need the Chamber on your side. As you grow, I'd suggest joining your State Chamber as well. Talk about powerful networking!

Look for young/professional groups, clubs, or organizations centered around a topic that interests you. Look into a Rotary group (or a similar group) that works on service projects. You could even join a non-profit board or event committee so you can meet and mingle with other folks in the community. You need to become a professional networker, because until you are Bill Gates, you need to "sell" your company to anyone and everyone. Let them know what you do and how they can get involved. Look on community calendars and go to anything and everything you possibly can.

Once we had gotten established and had more budget, I carved out funds to beef up networking. I joined new groups each year, and

More online:

tried to target (and retarget) the people I met. I applied for a leadership program in my town called Leadership Lexington, a year-long program with fifty-five other people, that dug deeper into the various industries and inner workings of our town. This program had *such* a powerful impact, and I found it an excellent use of my time and money. It led to some serious relationship building, and it plugged me into a large alumni network. I have stayed involved in it to this day, and I've continued generating business from it. The alumni view me as the "go-to" event producer in Kentucky. Be on the lookout for groups like this as you develop your company and your budget.

You might ask, "Okay, how do you network at an event?" Personally, I hit up the bar, first thing. Sometimes I need a little liquid courage before I work a room. (Don't get drunk, though—don't be that person.) Always bring business cards, and take opportunities to pass them out. Dress nicely, and don't take a bulky bag. Most importantly, be prepared to listen. If you really want to network well, listen just as much as you talk, if not more. The closer you listen, the more useful information you'll pick up. For instance, you hear about someone's work on something similar to your plans, and you realize you need to hire them for your next project. I've picked up tons of useful information by listening to other people. When I listen more than I speak, I engage better, and more people want to work with me as a result.

Let's say you meet someone who has just started a business. They want to get the word out about their product, service, or location. You can help by promoting their social accounts, sharing their business information, or sending potential customers their way. You might meet someone who sits on a non-profit board and needs to find auction items for an upcoming event. Maybe you can donate a product or recommend companies that do. If you do this often enough, eventually someone will ask you for a proposal for your product or service.

People want to work with someone they like—so be likeable. You'll get more openness to your business discussions if people feel like you give a shit about theirs. So give a shit. For about five years, I attended a quarterly networking event. I never pitched anyone; I simply enjoyed the event and meeting people who attended. In the third year, I kept running into a woman I knew loosely through the business community. She kept re-introducing herself to me, and at the end of every conversation she'd say, "I'm going to find a reason to hire you for an event!" I never pitched myself or my company. Instead, I asked questions about her family, her clients, and her projects. I was genuinely interested in her, and I never thought we'd have a reason to work together. I didn't feel the urge to "sell" her... but true to her word, she found a reason to hire us, and she remains one of our biggest clients to date.

You won't succeed at networking if you succumb to shyness. Even introverts must find ways to pretend to be extroverted—at least when it comes to introductions. I always try to find one person I already know in the room. I talk to them first to break the ice. Once I feel a bit more comfortable and have the lay of the land, I go and find someone I don't know and strike up a conversation. If it's a seated event with open seating, find a table where at least 75% of the folks sitting at the table are people you don't know. There is *no* point in paying for an event or spending time attending one to sit with a table full of people you already know. (Unless, of course, you've been invited by those people to attend for free—then you should sit with them.) Give a firm handshake; look people in the eyes. Introduce yourself (with your first *and* last name) and tell them the name of your company. They will follow suit, and you can take it from there.

I always have a couple of questions teed up if the conversation stalls or feels awkward.

- What does your company do?
  (Only use this if you truly don't know.)
- How did you get into this business?
- Any exciting projects you've been working on lately?
- How long have you been there?
- What brought you to XYZ company?
- What has been going well for you lately?
- What is not going so well?
- What are you looking forward to?

INCEPTION:
MEDIA

03 | **BUILD A BRAND**
DESIGN
WEBSITES
F*CKING SOCIAL MEDIA
PR & MARKETING
TRADEMARKS & PATENTS

Chapter Extras

Build a Brand

Lexington has a popular ice cream shop called Crank & Boom Ice Cream Company. Their craft ice cream brand and shop has multiple locations. Today, they ship their ice cream across the country. Like most small businesses, Crank & Boom evolved over the years. They originally grew out of a restaurant called Thai Orchid Cafe, where the owners served a small selection of rotating ice cream flavors. The owner, Toa, told me she bought a small ice cream maker and experimented with ice cream flavors, because she wanted to mix up the normal red bean and green tea ice cream they served in the past. Eventually, customers forgot about the Thai food and came mainly for the ice cream, and they wanted to buy it in bulk!

Toa knew she'd landed on something special. Once ice cream sales outpaced the restaurant's receipts, Toa made the leap to launch Crank & Boom. Because she decided to launch it as a stand-alone brand, the name "Thai Orchid Cafe" no longer worked. The ice cream did so well that she eventually closed the restaurant to narrow her focus.

Toa exudes the Crank & Boom brand everywhere she goes. It's more than kick-ass ice cream; it's a brand that loves and serves its community. Crank & Boom uses locally-sourced ingredients, supports local vendors, and gives back to the community. They're synonymous with friendly people who smile. Their product is craft and small batch, but with big soul and a lot of heart—all at the same time. I love how their company acts and makes you feel. Their logo and image match their spirit; they feel like "love on paper."

Crank & Boom has done a great job at carefully selecting their involvement in the community, without overwhelming themselves. They want to ensure their activities align with their brand and core values. For example, they have a small batch ice cream program where a portion of sales from specific club creams goes towards a new local non-profit each month. These groups make a big impact in the community. At one point, they had launched several retail locations, private events, a sister company, and a podcast. After COVID, they returned to their roots, stuck to the things they excelled at, and let go of the rest.

You must build a brand… not just a company. This brand needs to be nimble and mobile, flowing naturally everywhere you go. Create a brand your target customers can embrace. A brand means more than a logo, though it certainly includes that. It also encompasses your company motto, the values you stand for, how you communicate with clients and employees, and what type of business you conduct. This brand defines you and your company, so take time in the beginning to do it wholeheartedly.

To build a successful brand, ask yourself these serious questions, and take time to think about the answers:

- What do we believe in?

- What is our objective? (Think "mission statement")

- What culture do we aim to create in our workplace?

- What type of business do we want to create?

- How does our product or service benefit people?

- What is our impact in the world?

- What demographics will we cater our product/service to?

- How will they access our product/service?

- How do we want to communicate with our clients/customers? With our team?

You need to answer these questions to truly understand who your company will become. Then you can start working on the other pieces, like a logo or design. If you're still feeling uncertain, you might start with who you are not. Take my current company, Kentucky Event Company, for example:

- We are not inattentive to detail. We know that the small things matter.

- We do not leave clients to fend for themselves. We act as their backstop, their buffer, and protect them when it comes to their events.

- We do not cut corners or skimp on small things to save a few bucks. We also do not spend just because the budget is there.

- We do not settle for "okay." If the linen isn't straight or the graphics aren't right—we fix it.

BRANDING NOTES

More online:

You can discover a core part of knowing who you "are" by identifying who you are not.

Design

When I started LexEffect Events, I needed a logo and I wasn't sure where to turn. I didn't feel like I had the money to invest in a company to create a brand for us, and I didn't think we needed one. I thought, "I can do it myself," right?

Wrong! I had zero graphic design skills and no desire (or time) to learn, so I found a website called 99logos.com. In theory, you were supposed to provide them with an idea of what you wanted, and then freelance designers from around the world would bid on your project. From the art samples they produced, you picked your favorite. Then you paid $99, and the logo was yours.

Here is the logo I purchased for my company:

After we selected our designer, I asked him to change the colors from yellow to green and add a subtext line before we finalized the deal. He agreed and said he would make the changes once we completed the

transaction. I paid the fee … but then he took the money, sent us the same logo without the changes, and disappeared, never to be heard from again. The graphics were terrible. They had poor resolution, and the designer only gave us a few file types, so we couldn't use them anywhere without pixellation. We purchased it through an anonymous designer, so we had no point of contact if we ever needed anything updated or changed after the initial transaction. (Apparently this was in the website's fine print, which I failed to fully read and understand.)

We got screwed! I've since paid thousands to have this logo redrawn and adjusted so we can actually use it. I spent as much money re-creating the logo as I would have if I'd hired a company to do it right the first time! Here's how my branding looks today:

Once you create your company and brand, you get to do the fun part. Design is the next step in the media process, and it includes anything you might put your logo and brand on. Business cards, rack cards, collateral, marketing, advertising, your website, social media pages—it all needs a good design to match the brand you created. Make it cohesive across all platforms so when folks go from your website to your business card to a social media page, it all belongs to the same company. Please, for the love of all things small business, do not put pixelated, blurry images out into the world to represent your company. And please don't use cheesy stock images—especially with watermarks or logos from another company. It's already hard enough to be a small start-up business introducing yourself to the public. Don't cut yourself off at the knees by appearing cheap. You have two options: (a) hire someone to create these items for you or (b) learn graphic design and do it yourself.

Hiring someone to do it for you

I'm a firm believer that you should know what you're good at and stick to it. I am not good at design, the programs that come with it, or even drawing, for that matter. I believe you should always have logos designed by professionals. I'm sure you know someone who "does it on the side," or you've found a cheap online website, or some other inexpensive solution that sounds like a good idea… but it's not. Run away. Hire a professional to do professional work. When you look at a shoddy, unkempt website with misspelled words and outdated and pixelated photos, how do you feel? Wouldn't you doubt the quality of the content? You can find good graphic design firms with reasonably priced options for logo design. Do some research and hire one. Trust me—it's worth the time and money to get it right the first time.

Doing it yourself

When it comes to social media, online images, or graphics, I believe you can save time and money by doing them yourself. You'll need to learn the basics of Photoshop, InDesign, Illustrator, Canva, or other apps or programs, but you can get the basics down and create decent images. You also have the option of a graphic design intern who helps pro bono, for a small fee, or for a reference letter and experience. You still need to have high-resolution, good-quality images, but social media posts happen so frequently that it can become costly to pay a professional for this service on an ongoing basis.

I judge anyone with blurry or pixelated images on their social media accounts. I hesitate to hire any company that displays them. We live in a world where some folks may never visit your website… but they do check out your social media platforms. They judge you by this content, so make it count. In fact, we have some clients who never visit our website during the entire time we work with them. But they can tell me, to the second, what date and time we post something on social media.

After more than a decade as a business owner, I purposefully engage professionals to design all of our logos. Design matters, and we need consistency across all of our pages. We use the same fonts, colors, and copy everywhere. We use the same headers, formatting, and style. Why? Because we're a professional company, and we show up for our clients in this dependable way. We need prospective clients to observe and sense the same tone, style, and effort in everything we do. We want people to feel confident we'll give their business the same treatment.

Websites

Can you think of a time when you visited a poorly coded, templated website? You can tell by looking—they still have Latin filler text, graphics and logos have block backgrounds that don't match the site, they use twelve different fonts, and you can't find contact information anywhere. After seeing this site, how would you view this business? Would you want to work with them? Our first website was created by a friend of a friend, and viewers felt pretty skeptical about us. The colors didn't match our logo, and sometimes they didn't even match each other. The "tone" changed from page to page, the site had far too many tabs, and it was a mess. It felt bulky, it looked pixelated, and showcased its cheapness. People couldn't find what they wanted, and we looked like a rookie company that had no clue what we were doing. (To be clear, we were rookies.)

Your website is one of the most important pieces of collateral you create in the early stages of business. Social media is important too, but your website is a hub for information and communication. Most business transactions happen online, and people research and browse your website before picking up the phone to talk to you. A bad site can do more damage to your brand than not having a website at all. Here are a few important rules for building an effective website:

Pick an easy-to-remember URL

We named Lexington Event Company (now Kentucky Event Company) in order to maximize results from search engine optimization (SEO). The name tells you exactly what we do and where we're located. It's pretty simple. When people search for "event planner in Lexington" or "event planner in Kentucky," we always pop up at the top of the results.

If you can go with your company name, by all means do it. But if you have an awkward, confusing, or potentially misleading company name, maybe consider other URLs. Think about the nature of your product or service—

what will people type in a search engine to try and find you? LexEffect was an event management company based in Lexington, so possible searches included:

- Lexington event planning
- Kentucky event planning
- Lexington events
- Lexington entertainment
- entertainment Lexington
- wedding planner Lexington
- Kentucky meeting planner

We bought twelve versions of these URLs and linked them to the LexEffect website. This increased traffic and put us closer to the top in results when people searched for those phrases. Use GoDaddy.com or another domain purchasing website to see the available URLs. I suggest sticking with a dot-com URL—people don't regularly search for the others. Avoid hyphens or special characters in your domain name. Don't make it too long, and don't try to be too creative or fancy. No one searches for "my-company-name-is-number-one.com." Think about what potential customers search for. We actually struggled with the name "LexEffect"—everyone always wanted to add an "s" on the end. They'd type in LexEffects.com, and they couldn't find us. Someone already owned the URL www.lexeffect.com, so we had to go with lexeffectky.com, which wasn't the automatic choice for folks putting it into a search engine.

You may need additional hosting (depending on where you buy the URL), and/or a website template. Hold off on purchasing any of these additional items until you have the domain figured out; you can always go back and change it later. Add an email address to this URL; please don't use a Gmail, Yahoo, or Hotmail email address for your business, unless you mask it. GoDaddy.com has an easy system to use when starting out, and it's free or reasonably priced, depending on the other services you add. I have a hard time taking seriously people who contact me with a gmail.com address they made in high school and want to charge large fees for products or services. You're running a business. Stop it.

Creating a website

Once you've set up your domain, create your website. Take your time and do it right. You may find this an expensive and time-consuming process. You're going to have a big push for your initial launch, so you want the website to be user-friendly, accurate, and functional the first time anyone sees it.

You can hire a website developer or create your own using a template. There are pros and cons to both options. If you need a complex website with multiple pages and customizations, but the site doesn't need regular updates, hire someone to create it for you. If you don't have time to learn WordPress or HTML coding, pay someone to do it. Ask the web developer to give you access to certain areas of the website for minor updates you can do on your own. Either do that, or work out a deal for a low hourly rate for edits or updates as you go.

If your website will be simple and you need regular updates, I suggest creating and managing it yourself. LexEffect did both: our main company website (created and managed by an outside company) and our individual event websites (created and managed by us). On event websites, we needed hourly updates, especially during peak event times and seasons. We had trouble completing them on time, especially for the cost (equivalent to a full-time salary) in website maintenance fees. We understood our web maintenance providers couldn't drop everything immediately to update a ticket link or adjust a sponsor logo. But we also couldn't put things on hold for a week-long turnaround, so we found ways to do it ourselves.

If you create your own website and know nothing about HTML or coding, I highly recommend SquareSpace or a similar website template platform. I am SquareSpace's self-proclaimed ambassador, and I cannot sing their praises enough. Their platform allows you to pick through templates and create a website with drag-and-drop features. It's easy to use, and you can change your website and template as often as you want. Your purchase price includes website hosting, and you can link it to your own URL and save hundreds of dollars in hosting fees. They have a very user-friendly e-commerce option as well. Squarespace isn't the only option. You can find many choices, so do some research and find out what works best for you. For us, this route saves us a ton of money and time. It helps us earn more money, and it raises our profile and online presence quite a bit. Since writing this, we've moved all of our company websites to SquareSpace platforms, and we manage them in-house. I'm still a believer!

Mobile Friendly

Any website you create must be mobile-friendly. This is a requirement, not a suggestion. With our events and clients, over 80% of traffic comes from mobile activity. You want to think holistically about where your customers come from and how they find you. If it's complicated to find information or convert a sale

Website URL Ideas

on their phone, customers will not make an effort to come back the next time they sit in front of a computer. Most templates are "mobile compatible," but take the time and make sure. Check every page, link, and button to see how it shows up on a smartphone. You may have to re-format the way the site shows up for the mobile version while the site's integrity stays the same for a computer. Fix all the bugs before launching. Consider this your digital "grand opening." Would you invite people to your grand opening or ribbon cutting with unfinished walls and floors? (I hope the answer is "No.")

Links, Images, and Video

The first thing people see on your landing page needs to intrigue them enough to linger. Make your logo visible, and show your brand and product. If you convert sales directly from your website (e.g., event ticket sales), make sure people can find where to purchase within the first ten seconds of viewing your page. They don't want to waste time or energy searching for hidden links to their next step, so make it easy for them.

Test all links and make sure they <u>open in a new window or tab</u>. Anything that changes the screen to a new site takes them away from yours, which defeats the purpose. Link to other places on your website as necessary, but don't constantly send people down rabbit trails.

Images attract viewers, but words get better SEO rankings. You want striking images, but use your words, too. Videos can be

helpful sometimes, but I hate any website that automatically plays videos or sound bites. First of all, they're annoying. No one wants to be that girl in a coffee shop that has the sound turned to 100%, and the Barry White song comes on automatically, and suddenly everyone stares at you. Secondly, I shouldn't have to update Java and download some plug-in to browse your website. Don't add anything to your site that slows the upload/download because of internet speed. Make videos, recordings, and photo albums optional.

Always, always have a contact form. Give folks the opportunity to get in touch if they have questions. And please—provide contact information. When you list your contact information, leave "spaces" in your email address so it doesn't get spammed. Spell it like this:

kaelyn@ emailaddress.com

If you don't want to list your email, at least provide a phone number or some way for visitors to reach you. People shouldn't have to fill out twelve-question contact forms and then wait to hear back from you for simple questions or to get in touch. And for goodness' sake, _respond_ when people contact you through your website.

Updates and Maintenance

If you want your website to optimize (show up at the top of search engines), it needs regular updates and maintenance. Make sure you have tags and keywords coded in your pages—good words (but not fluff words) that the internet "spiders" can find to help optimize your page. Pages should have titles and subtitles that explain the content they display. Keep your site clean and simple, but refresh it periodically to get a better SEO rating. Google reviews and other third-party review sites also help with this, and blogs can give a great boost with regular content (although you have to keep up with them). Always check links to ensure they haven't broken, as well as updates to calendars, business hours, and contact information. Don't lose potential business because a client or customer used a broken link or outdated information. Keep these things fresh by showcasing your work! Add case studies, recap a recent project, or debrief a recent engagement. It shows people what you can do and improves your SEO ranking.

F*cking Social Media

If you saw some of my social media posts from early in my career, you would shudder. You might even wonder why I didn't delete them, set my phone on fire, and change my name. They are that bad. I used pixelated images, stock photos, weird phrasings, and an inconsistent voice. When Instagram launched and allowed business pages, I would sometimes (accidentally) post personal things on my business page… cringe! Even as recently as writing this book, I realized I had done this and went back and deleted more of them (double cringe).

Social media is one of the easiest ways to promote your business when you start. In the old days, before phones had fancy cameras (and before we learned how to use them well), before we could hire professional photographers to shoot our events, and before we knew how the hell social media worked—we winged it, and it was not good. When I mistakenly posted something personal on my social media page, suddenly, all our business followers knew about my weekend plans, things I liked and didn't like, and plenty of useless information they didn't care to know. (Remember when we used to post status updates like we send texts?! Whyyyyyy????)

If you really want second-hand embarrassment, let me tell you about a time I lied and told a client I couldn't meet with them because I had another client meeting. I actually had other personal plans, but in those days I wasn't firm in my boundaries with clients, and I felt bad about taking time off. It felt wrong to tell a client "no" to a meeting when I had a personal commitment already on the calendar. So, after telling them I was committed to another client meeting, I posted a photo on Instagram (on our business page!) of me and my college sorority sisters "meeting" at a concert. Big oops.

A decade ago, the only social media platform for business was Facebook. You could have a very simple page to display contact info, make updates, and add photos. No one offered reels, threads, feeds, or tagging. Life felt simpler, and we spent less time planning our social media calendars because we didn't have them. Today, social media offers both the best… and the worst. You have an ideal place to show visuals of your product or service—but it requires 24/7 monitoring. The "rules" constantly change, and you have to work hard to keep up with trends. Social media management is now a literal full-time job.

Social media is THE WORST (have I said that enough?). It slowly consumes our lives, to the point that most people today live and die by it. Companies reallocated advertising budgets and reorganized marketing roadmaps to account for social media management and the new audience of online viewers. It's a huge rabbit hole of information, and the only rule is that there are no "rules"—but also, there are all the rules, all at once. And the rules change. Every platform reaches a different audience through its own set of algorithms. You benefit if you use it well, but having social media accounts without using them will give you worse results than not having accounts at all. And just because you know how to post pictures of your dog on your personal account doesn't make you a master of social business pages.

Just when I think I've figured out the new Facebook algorithm, we hear from the twenty-somethings that Facebook is for old people! Now, we use X, formerly known as Twitter. X is fun, except that, unless you pay for a premium account, you can only write 140 characters. How the hell can you explain things in 140 characters?! With X you have to post ALL THE TIME, because it's a constant, running feed of others' thoughts. It doesn't format photos well, so you must have the perfect text. To be relevant, you have to post, post, post!

At the time of writing this, Instagram has shifted to attract a younger audience, and it's 100% photo-driven. You can post the same content on Facebook and Instagram, but you need to make each site feel organic. Otherwise, it gets boring and old. Instagram recently added reels, so now, for your account to stay relevant (and feed the algorithm), you must post reels 3-5 times a week. Then Meta came up with Threads —I don't even know what Threads is, and I refuse to learn! I refuse to engage in TikTok—my brain can't handle any more charts or schedules, rules or calendars. And what ever happened to Vines?!

It's overwhelming—and I'm a (self-taught) social media manager. I'll share what I know:

- You should have the same handle on all of your social media platforms (or as similar as possible, based on what's available). Think again about what people search for. Don't try to be clever; you'll miss out on potential business. (Example: LexEffect or LexEffectKY, not LexPartyPrincess or KYPartyPlanner)

- Put clean, crisp images and logos on your profiles and posts. Most people come to your social media pages right after (if not before) looking at your website, so don't skimp on this. (We have clients who've never visited our website and only go to our socials for information and to vet us as a potential vendor).

- Make sure your brand shows through and you have uniformity across all your platforms. See previous section regarding consistency. This means the same colors, fonts, copy, voice, and so on.

A few things I've learned about the more popular social media platforms:

Facebook has a reputation as one of the most commonly used platforms. The rules change often, so you have to keep up with new algorithms and plugins to make sure your efforts actually make a difference for your business. Facebook's audience has shifted a little—posts and ads gear towards an older, majority-female demographic. We use Facebook for "pitchy," sales-type posts, along with links to articles, videos, and event pages. Interactions look different than on other platforms, so if you need people clicking links or want them to "share" something, Facebook is your best bet.

The 80/20 Rule: if you constantly post sales pitches, people will unfollow you. Post sales-y content no more than 20% of the time. For the other 80%, mix in business-related posts, community stories, articles, and videos—content relevant to your industry or city that is non-sales or self-promotion. This keeps people interacting with your page and keeps the annoyance level at a minimum. In Lexington, sports-related posts work well, especially if it's for the University of Kentucky. We also get good reception for community events and a fair return on industry-related trends, articles, or videos. We post recaps of our events, including photos and event stats. Lastly, we share links to our website blog where we include tips and tricks for events and event businesses. It gives readers industry information that might be useful to them, and it brings them to our website where they might explore past the blog.

Blogs allow us to write longer posts about topics or issues that interest our audience. There's no point writing a three-page Facebook post—

Facebook won't allow it, and no one would read it. But you can post a teaser on Facebook with a link to your website, where viewers can find an in-depth post. We write blog posts with tips, tricks, how-tos, and advice for events. How do we come up with these posts? We write about topics and incidents happening in our business at that time. We answer questions our clients ask. We discuss issues we deal with during events. We don't call out names or give away sensitive information, but if clients deal with contracting issues, we write posts about contracts. If we work with a number of food and beverage clients, we'll do an entry like "5 Things to Remember When Creating Your Food & Beverage Plan."

Recently, I wrote a blog about event signage. We had several clients in the final stages of planning, and signage sat on the top of everyone's mind. I provided the same list of FAQs about signage to four different clients, and I thought, "If these clients all have the same questions, I bet other people do, too." So we wrote a blog post, added it to social media with a link, and invited people to contact us free of charge if they wanted to talk through their signage plan. Two people took me up on the offer, and I sent an email with some thoughts about signage. One hired

Social Media Notes

More online:

us to coordinate their event. They later revealed that they struggled with planning and needed professional help.

Facebook doesn't optimize anything that leads you away from their site, so you need to make shortened URLs for article links, videos, blogs, etc. Images engage better than text, so always have some type of visual to add to your post. Facebook also has an algorithm (as of writing this book) that "buries" your posts in followers' feeds if they haven't interacted with your page at least once every thirty days. The 80/20 rule can help with this. Post something that asks people to "like" if they agree, or "share" if they're excited, and so on. This encourages them to interact with your page, and they'll also see your future posts.

A good business social media user follows the rules about how often and when to post on Facebook. Your local SBDC should have social media classes. I suggest taking these courses as often as you can; you'll always learn something new. Just because something works well for Company A doesn't mean Company B will get the same result. Facebook lets you see the statistics of when your posts hit peak performance, your audience demographics, what types of posts optimize best on your page, the best days and times to post based on your followers, and more. Look at these stats and use them to your benefit.

You can pay to promote your page, website, a post or an event. The nice thing about Facebook advertising is that you can set a budget that works for you—anything from $10 to $1000 will get traction on your page. I recommend Facebook advertising, but be smart about it. Use it to build momentum and awareness, but only for important messages. If you promote every post, people get annoyed. Consider your best posts, the day and time you posted them, and try to mimic that pattern with ads.

Pro tip: Pay ongoing attention to these ads. Don't "set it and forget it." Every May, we help promote a craft beer festival. We manage the marketing and promotion for the series, while the brewers produce their own events. Our marketing budget covers digital, print, and social ads. Last year, I ran ads and failed to check on them. A whole month after the event ended, I was still getting charged by Facebook. The ad had toggled to a "daily" limit with unlimited days, instead of a "budget limit" that programmed it to turn off once that limit was hit. We unknowingly spent the full budget on Facebook ads—after we had already spent the budget on our original marketing plan. Several thousands of dollars over-budget later… I won't make that mistake again!

Finally, if you're going to schedule Facebook posts (which you should), schedule these directly on Facebook and not through a platform program (like Hootsuite). Facebook doesn't like outside "programs," and they don't always convert the way they should. It's a pain in the ass, but you'll find it worth the extra step. Now Meta owns both Facebook and Instagram, you can seamlessly cross-post between these two platforms.

Twitter/X. In my humble opinion, X is the hardest social media platform to use, retain traction, and convert sales—at least for my industry. Every millisecond, somebody posts something new. You have to post nonstop to engage with your consumer. If that isn't enough, each time you post, you need something new, witty, and fresh to keep their attention. X users are mostly male, ages eighteen to thirty-five. That is the demographic of our typical X follower, and they look for quick interactions and immediate responses.

In contrast to Facebook, X is best managed through a scheduling platform, like Hootsuite. Schedule several posts each day, in weekly blocks. You can always plug in real-time posts, but pre-filling your feed helps fill content and

time. Keep in mind, X requires user-heavy attention; the only way to make this platform work for you is if you are able to regularly check in and interact with your followers. You should respond, favorite, or re-tweet almost anything a follower posts to you, for you, or about you. This keeps the momentum going and increases organic traffic.

Instagram. At the time of writing, Instagram is one of the world's most popular social media platforms. Any posts you promote on Facebook will also show up on Instagram. It operates as a "real-time" platform. You can plug in created images or "selling" posts, but it works better for real-time photo and video updates. We use Instagram for in-person activity, such as employee outings, lunch at a sponsor's restaurant, shopping for a farm-to-table dinner at the farmers market, or event pictures and footage. You will get the most traction on Instagram this way.

URLs do not hyperlink on Instagram, so you need to update the website link in your bio (or profile). Video posts are sixty seconds or less, so make it count! With Instagram, the key is great visuals. Don't put blurry or dark images on your page! Take time, use a filter, and make it worth stopping to look and read more. We try to keep content differentiated between our posts and our stories. You'll come across arguments for both ways as to which is more important or gains more traction. And, of course, the algorithm changes constantly, so you have to keep up with the evolving "rules."

LinkedIn – You should have a personal LinkedIn account already. If you don't, stop what you're doing right now and make one. Why? It provides a great way to network virtually, especially business-to-business. You can easily connect with business people who might want to use your products or services, announce business news, list available jobs, internships, or contract positions, and ask industry related questions. A LinkedIn profile elevates the professionalism of your new company, and it gives others the impression you have a well established and connected operation.

With all forms of social media (for any who think I'm not serious about this), make sure you have high-resolution, good-quality images and logos on your business account. I won't take seriously any company with a blurry, pixelated image with improper sizing. Find out the dimensions of the page and put the correct image there. (And yes, I know I was that company at one time—but we evolve, people!)

We regularly get business referrals from Linkedin. On both my personal page and the business page, content occasionally overlaps, but we try to keep it fresh. The business page focuses on event recaps, tips & tricks, industry trends, and advice for planning events. On my personal page, I post about projects, upcoming events, community endeavors I'm involved in, and general advice.

YouTube – If you have promotional videos, recaps, virtual tours, or anything similar, a YouTube channel is essential. YouTube (like Vimeo) is a place to house the videos, but you can easily connect to a website, social media, and other locations on the web. This gives you additional tags on the internet, which helps with SEO. Like with images, a YouTube channel still reflects your company, so don't put a bad quality video online and expect to get traction.

In the beginning, we partnered with a videographer who wanted to grow his business. He gave us good quality videos on a quick turnaround for a low price, in exchange for having his logo in the video and our commitment to tag him when we posted them. We could afford it, we promoted him, and we got better-than-iPhone videos we could use for our own marketing and advertising. Keep in mind—if you have a large-scale production or need a specific kind of video (e.g: MoonTower

Great Ideas

Music Festival), you need a bigger production group to manage that project. Some things require the expense.

Blogs/News Feeds – If you like writing and you want to share detailed information, or if you have tips and ideas to give customers, you can effectively use blogs and feeds to do it. Like other forms of social media, you can benefit greatly from blogs and feeds if you use them properly.

- Post regularly. Posting 1-3 times per month works well, and it gives you content to feed into other social platforms. If you have enough content to post once a week—even better. Having a blog and not using it is like having pancakes without butter… Why would you do that?

- Use keywords relevant to the topic of the blog and to your industry. This helps make your blog post and website searchable, and improves your website's SEO ranking. Make sure you use similar words throughout the blog post, as well, so the internet finds the post.

- Use good images. People don't want to read three pages-worth of text. Give them something visual. Don't steal images; that's called plagiarism or copyright infringement, and you can't do that without consequences. Sure, you could easily Google a picture or image relevant to your topic, but if you ignore my advice and steal pictures off the internet—at least be smart enough to use images without a copyright. Also, don't use images with watermark phrases on them… You can search on free sites, like Pexels or Unsplash, where you can download quality images. We found freelance photographers trying to start their businesses and paid a small fee to get photos of our events.

We like to add contact forms and Q&A boxes at the end of blog posts to encourage feedback, interaction, and easy access to reach us if readers want to know more.

Email Lists – One of the most important (and easy) methods you can use to help build your social profile and contact list is an email database. We use MailChimp (which is free until you hit a certain number of emails), and we love it. Every time someone buys a product, becomes a client, purchases a ticket (or whatever fits with your company), add them to your email list—with permission, of course. Sending a once-or-twice-monthly email blast with upcoming details, sales, events, industry trends, links to your blog, and so on will help keep people connected.

As with social media, look at your demographics and statistics (every email platform has this plug-in option) to make sure you send emails on the right days and times. During my LexEffect days, we never sent more than one-to-two email blasts per month to avoid annoying people. This means you have to plan content based on your calendar and events. Spend time on these emails, use good images, double check links, and give it a good read-through before sending. As we've mentioned several times, if someone clicks on a link and it's broken, they most likely won't bother to find the information another way, which means you lose the potential sale. Make it easy and visual.

PR & Marketing

Marketing, advertising, and public relations are valuable to any business, but getting them right is tricky. They usually take up a lot of budget, and the two million options you can use to promote your company are overwhelming. So first, let's cover some definitions:

Marketing – the action or business of promoting and selling products or services, including market research

Advertising – the activity or profession of producing advertisements for commercial products or services (radio, TV, or newspaper ads)

Public Relations (PR) – the practice of managing the spread of information between an individual/organization and the public.

To get attention and convert a sale in my industry requires a "five-touch" system. That means someone needs to see my brand/ad/promotion at least five times before they convert into a customer. When a potential client contacts us for the first time, we get some initial information. One of the questions we ask is "How did you hear about us?" Our two largest sources of business are referrals and search engines. Either a past client tells someone to call us, or they search for something like "event planner kentucky" or "wedding planner louisville" on the internet. Almost without fail, they say: "Then I went to your website, or xyz social media platform, and looked at your content, your reviews, etc., and knew you'd be a good fit!" The remaining 5% of clients find us from a social media post, article, or ads in a magazine. But they too go to our website or social media to learn more before they contact us.

Each industry has different parameters, which means you need a good marketing mix. Starting out, use every free avenue available to promote your business. For example, we focused on social media, community calendars, TV and radio interviews, fliers, handbills, and other free or low-cost methods of marketing and advertising. As you grow, add forms of paid promotion that

Great Ideas

reach people outside your normal channels. I'll warn you – this requires trial and error. You never know exactly what works best for your company. You can do as much research as possible and ask all your marketing friends, but in the end, your business will have different needs and outcomes than anyone else. So, trust your gut, remain cautious with spending money, and, sometimes, just take a leap.

Marketing – Most business owners don't market strategically, which means you need a strategy. Even as you navigate through trial and error, this doesn't mean "throwing spaghetti at the wall and seeing what sticks." Plan this out, and understand that it takes time. Sit down and sketch out the following:

Who do you want to reach?
Who is your target customer?

Zero in on the customer you want to receive your messaging, and you'll narrow down where that message goes.

Plan out social media first, including holidays and specials.

Once you know what that schedule looks like, decide what your marketing mix will be. Radio, TV, print, billboards, digital ads, promotional products, sponsorships, email and snail mail ads all work as great forms of marketing and advertising. Bear in mind, you might not have the budget for all of them at first, and not every form fits everyone, all the time.

Figure out the strategies that make sense for each specific marketing method, and your monthly budget. This schedule will change along with your business, so prepare to be flexible when you need to adjust your plans.

Advertising – Once you know your target customer and schedule, decide how you plan to reach them. You can advertise in many ways and places, but you have to make sure you get your money's worth if you pay for ads.

The first step is to create good quality ads. You might as well not bother, instead of running a poor-quality TV ad. If you must use TV, partner with a station that can help you produce the ad in their studio. Check the ratings and demographics of the station to make sure it reaches your target audience.

How will you measure the response to your ads? Will customers need to use a code at checkout? Do you ask them how they heard about your product or service? Tracking responses isn't the easiest thing in the world, but if you don't set up a system to capture whatever data you can, you'll never know if your methods are effective. We ask every new client at their first consultation how they heard about us. That tells us where to focus or multiply our advertising efforts.

Public Relations – This comes into play more once you are well-established, but never miss an opportunity to tell people what you're up to —or how it's succeeding. You could make an announcement about hiring a new employee, launching a new product, or introducing a community service initiative. A simple press release helps to spread the word, and if it's a good topic, you could get some attention from local or industry media. Check your local Chamber of Commerce, networking groups, magazines and business publications. Most have opportunities to list updates and "press information" for free. Strategic public relations opportunities, if done well, can create more buzz around your new business and increase awareness and curiosity. There are plenty of freelance PR professionals, along with stand-alone agencies, that offer these services. Look into them, even if just to tuck their information away for later when you have the funds to engage them.

After we closed LexEffect and opened Lexington Event Company, I launched a podcast. Podcasts were booming, and this method allowed another way for me to speak to my audience (literally) and provide more insight on topics than the traditional blog post. I found a site where you could record, edit, and host a podcast with little experience or equipment. The episodes were decent quality, and I featured different guests on a number of topics. The podcast explored the ups and downs of business ownership, largely following the outline of this book.

I felt like I wanted to say and explore more than I could put into writing. I knew several other business owners (or future ones) struggling with the same issues I faced. The podcast gave me an an opportunity to talk through those issues—if only so other business owners realized they weren't alone in the journey. It was a hit, and I had so much fun creating it.I found it resonated with many small business owners who related to the content.

When COVID hit, we pivoted to talk about mandates and restriction updates in our area and the struggles and stressors of business ownership during the pandemic. Big Ideas, Small Business still releases new episodes today. I love having this outlet to talk (freely) about business issues, share what I'm going through, and discuss the work I'm already doing. It drives traffic to my sites and gives me content to post. Most of all, it's fun! It doesn't currently function as a revenue generating activity for me, so I don't stress over how often I post. When I have a topic I want to explore, a person I want to interview, or a great opportunity, I make it happen and post. Sometimes I go a month or so without posting. If and when I want to ramp up this tool, I'll post episodes more regularly.

Trademarks & Patents

Trademarks and patents are a catch-22. They're important, but easily defeated, and the trademark board regularly disputes them. You can't trademark common words, images, or phrases. You can't trademark anything that doesn't clearly represent your brand. And you'll find very few unique names and ideas anymore—there will likely be more than onew person trying to create the same company/product/service as you. My trademark attorney told me that trademarks are only as good as the person willing to pay the most to fight when people infringe upon them. We hold several trademarks for event concepts, names, logos, and more—and we have spent money defending those trademarks.

For example, we had a concept called "The Bourbon Social." Another group in Lexington tried to host an event with the same name (and general concept/agenda). Our attorney reached out and informed them that we had the trademark on the name and that they couldn't use it. They changed their marketing and called it something else, and we all moved on. That's the best-case scenario.

Elsewhere, my family owns a large restaurant group in the western U.S. They have had dozens of concepts over the years—bars, catering company, restaurants, clubs, a brewery. They've been very successful, which also makes them a target. Someone in Lexington opened two locations using the same name (and spelling) as one of my family's restaurants. They even offered some of the same menu items. I suppose they didn't expect that someone in Lexington was connected to the restaurant group in Colorado. Once we discovered it, my uncle and his attorney contacted the Lexington restaurant owner and informed them that they had the trademark on the name and didn't give permission for the use. They argued back and forth, but in the end, the name remained and my uncle decided to let it go. The cost to fight it was more than it was worth, especially across state lines. Eventually, the copycat restaurant went out of business.

In the end, the costs of a legal battle to defend a trademark tells you whether it's worth the effort. Get with your small business development representative to see whether you need a trademark or patent. Depending on what you want to protect, it may not be necessary or worth your time and money. At the end of the day, you'll have to pay an attorney to apply and defend a trademark or patent, so consider all the options. Learn your common law trademark rights and any other options that might exist while you build the company. You can always apply for a trademark or patent later, once you get things rolling.

Great Ideas

INVESTMENT:
FINANCES

04 | BUSINESS PLAN
RAISING FUNDS
LOANS vs. INVESTORS
BILLS and VENDORS

Chapter Extras

Business Plan

My business struggled frequently, and for a long time I didn't realize how bad it was. We had "cash flow," but we never seemed to have *money*. Lots of cash came in, but much more went out. Our resources stretched thin, and it felt like we were drowning. Because I wasn't fully paying attention to our profit-and-loss (P&L) statement, I missed several financial mistakes that could have been fixed to minimize the financial bleed.

One of my investors asked to meet and review the business plan and our financials. He asked about certain expenses, clients, and profit margins. He looked at the business plan and pointed out that our profit & loss statement didn't match our business plan. We hadn't followed it! We'd jumped off the tracks, and it showed. Right then, I had an "a-ha" moment. It never occurred to me to check in on the plan to make sure I still followed the path. Today, I teach this process to my entrepreneurship students.

You should always have a business plan for your company, stating (among other things) your targets for revenue and profit margin. Call it a roadmap, if you will. Write out what you want to do with your company: goals, processes, earnings, non-negotiable values, and company mission. Even if you only make it for yourself, a business plan helps you evaluate progress, remember your mission, and keep you focused. Your business plan should be updated regularly. As your business changes, so should your goals and direction.

Topics you should include:

- Business Risk(s)
- Mission Statement
- Location Details
- What is Your Business Purpose
- Research Summary of Your Industry
- Research on Competitors
- Employee Information (actual names if you have them, or your plan for hiring)
- Commitments, Missions, Philanthropy, etc. (if any)
- Financial Projections

If you plan to seek capital or financing:

- Deal Terms (if for investors)
- Potential Financial Projections
- 4-Year Profit and Loss Statements (projections)
- Letters of Reference (if applicable)
- Past Statements (if already a current business)
- Any other relevant data or information for the investment/financing reviewers

I suggest you review the plan once a year with investors or business advisors, and adjust it based on the ebbs and flows of your company.

When I created our first business plan, it was for my eyes only. I projected when I wanted to be in a position to hire employees, how many event productions we would own, and how much revenue I wanted to make. I now review and adjust the plan and goals regularly to make sure we have realistic expectations, goals to strive for, and a reasonable outlook on our company's status. I also adjust for missteps, loss of sales, and other hiccups along the way.

Have a mentor or business partner review your business plan, too. Fresh eyes, especially unbiased ones, are always a good thing.

The business plan today looks much different than when I started. It focuses more on our mission, who we want to work with, what we provide, and how we want to impact our clients and our community. It stresses the vision, direction, and desires of our team, and it outlines just as much about what we *won't* do and who we won't work with. (*Over the years, I've realized the importance of identifying what you don't want as much as*

what you want.) Our plan doesn't look like a traditional business plan. Since we don't have investors or partners, we don't need all the same pieces as others who have those financial elements to factor. We now have more of a "business road map" or "business mission."

Raising Funds

Raising capital sucks! Unless you're gifted at asking people for money, or have a team of people with unlimited funds ready to write a check, you're going to **hate** this part.

More online:

NOTES

You recall my frustrations with social media? This is even worse.

LexEffect grew to a point where we needed to raise capital. We had self-funded two festivals, and it was expansion time. We needed more—hands, and money. So we started the process to raise capital. I had no idea about the rollercoaster ride I was about to take—and how it would change the course of my life.

If you can run your business and build slowly without having to raise money, that's the best route. Raising capital takes an enormous amount of effort and time. And once you get the money, you obligate yourself to other people who expect a return. But if you can't run your business without capital, or if you've reached a point where growth requires some upfront cash… away you go!

First, to raise capital, you need that business plan. Make sure you've spent time working on yours. The folks at SBDC can help you create, edit, and format your plan—but trust me, you'd better know this thing inside and out. No matter who you go to for money, they will ask questions about it. They'll want answers to many tough questions, too, and you need to know everything about the business and the financials. If the bank or investor doesn't feel comfortable with your plan or your knowledge of the business, you can forget about getting money from them. You only get one shot with each person, so make it count.

I'm talking about more than just a plan for making money—your plan should explain how your company and industry work. Assume the person you talk to doesn't know anything about your industry. The investors I talked to wanted my business plan to describe "the deal," as well as the industry, our objectives, our processes, and the pathway to profitability for everyone.

Once you have your business plan ready and you know the details in depth, you need a list of people to approach. You'll find many options, and your financial advisors can help you decide what type of financing works best for your business. Each revenue source has pros and cons, so think it through carefully. Keep in mind that sometimes the best option, or the one that seems the best, won't be available to you. Don't get stuck on that; be flexible and adaptable. You're an entrepreneur, after all.

Loans vs. Investors

When we first sought to raise capital, I pitched to several banks. I thought I needed either a loan or line of credit. While I had to jump through hoops with applications and a deep dive of my finances, I had a good credit score. I had no issues with unpaid balances, and I figured this would prevent issues with a board of investors looming over my head. As I soon discovered, a two-year-old, service-based company with minimal collateral in a fluctuating industry that few bankers understood… does *not* make a prime candidate for a loan. An uncle once advised me *never* to use my house as collateral—to keep my personal assets separate from my business assets at all costs. So when I say I had "minimal collateral," I mean "zero." (*This advice came in handy years down the road when I had to file bankruptcy for a company. More on that later.*)

Banks care more about their risk and your ability to repay than about your cool idea, product, or service. As mentioned above, you can gain capital and financing through several avenues. Decide the right way for you, but know in advance that sometimes you have to adjust your expectations, and you won't find any guarantees. Look into several options, and get with your consultant and attorney to ensure that you have covered all your bases. Possible financing options to consider;

- Bank loan
- Bank line of credit (revolving)
- Angel investors
- Private investors (equity/capital)
- Private lenders
- Crowdsourcing or pre-sales

Pros and Cons vary from option to option, but it all depends on your circumstances. While some banks may not need you to report to a board, they usually have strict regulations. You'll most likely need some type of collateral and *great* credit history. Repayment terms are set, with interest; they offer very little flexibility and you cannot default.

Private investors are great because they invest in you, not necessarily your credit score or collateral. The downside is they're hard to find and require a lot of maintenance like keeping up with reports, meetings, and investor relations (and personalities—so many personalities). They typically function as long-term partners and want a great return, understandably. If you work with a private investor(s), you now answer to a person or group that owns part of your business and wants to ensure it runs as expected. Be prepared to answer tough questions when things fall short of expectations.

Work as many angles as you can so you have more than one option. Prior to getting capital, I self-funded the entire operation. Business revenues supported the difference, but we normally fell behind, and I didn't take a paycheck for the first three years. Although I wasn't in debt per se, the scarcity of cash delayed and prevented operations and growth. When we went to raise capital and I couldn't get a loan, we tried a different approach: a mix of private investors and a bank line of credit. This provided enough capital in our first round to hire an additional employee and enhance some of our events.

Before you seek financing, know the differences between loans and investors, and make sure you fully understand your deal. Don't forget that you repay loans (whether privately or with a bank) with interest. Lenders normally set repayment schedules within a set timeframe, and they can sometimes be renewable or revolving. Investors differ from lenders; investors normally hold equity (ownership) in your company, and do not receive a repayment of their investment amount. Rather, they receive a percentage of revenues (dividends) after a certain period, depending on the agreement. Both options have pros and cons, so make sure you know your needs and plan for the best way to achieve them. And of course there are other, less common methods of financing, such as loaning money to yourself against a retirement portfolio, or Infinite Banking, which uses a life insurance policy to build cash value. Both of these, of course, assume that you already have those tools in place and have built up wealth over time. They are not quick fixes.

You may have to get funds from more than one source to get the full amount you need, and you may need to run a second or third round to keep operations going. Be super-specific about how much money you need, what the money will be used for… and then double that total, because it's always more expensive than you think. With contracts, for example, it's better to get the terms "right" in advance of making the deal than pay attorneys to fix it later. (*Legal bills… that shit gets expensive.*)

List of Potential Investment Avenues

More online:

I once spent tens of thousands of dollars trying to get out of a bad investment deal. I worked with a real estate attorney who drafted the agreement (though he had little experience with this type of contract).

Pro tip: attorneys specialize, just like doctors. Just as you don't want your primary care physician operating on your heart, don't have a real estate attorney draft an operating agreement and investment deal. Mine worked with one of my potential investors to create this deal, and subsequent operating and subscription agreements. I am currently on my third attorney for this; I hired her to untangle the web the first attorney created (the second one refused to address it).

This mess led me to file bankruptcy for LexEffect Events. The original operating agreement promised investors 100% repayment within two years, plus 100% interest in years 3-4, and then an additional 2% of net revenue from the company in year five and beyond. The contract listed them as equity investors, but in reality they functioned as lenders. The operating agreement and the tax structure didn't match up. Doesn't that sound like a good repayment deal? It was certainly great for them! On paper, the offer was great, but in real life it was a complete disaster.

I made the payments the first year, but fell behind in the ensuing years when sales dropped or losses prevented me from paying. I later learned that the "investors"… weren't *really* investors. They were more like loan officers making a private loan—yet they came with the same maintenance and expectations a group of investors would. I used the wrong attorney to draft the plan, I didn't review it for tax purposes, and I blindly trusted the two people creating the plan without becoming knowledgeable myself. I made the biggest failure of my career and created the worst mess to clean up—*ever*. Not to mention the expense, stress, and anxiety that comes with filing bankruptcy for a company. Remember when I told you I did *not* use my house as collateral for a loan? Now you know why.

When I say "dealing with investors," let me explain what I mean: investors come with baggage. One investor got involved so he could get his son a job, and the son eventually quit. Another investor wanted to meet with me every week. She had dozens of business ideas she wanted help with, and at the time I didn't realize I could say "No" to these meetings. I spent a substantial amount of time with her talking about ideas for which I had neither time nor interest.

A third investor treated me like his personal assistant, and acted like he could do as he pleased with the business. He wanted to review and approve all clients before they came on board. He demanded we give his family free, all-access passes to every event we produced, and he also wanted me to run other "good ideas" in exchange for his financial commitment to the company.

"Quiet" investors aren't much better. Some of ours never engaged with us at all. When we told them we needed help, they pretended to not know who we were. One of them lived in a different state and demanded phone calls to review financials… and then didn't bother to answer the phone when we called for the scheduled time. He'd call back later—usually in the middle of an active event—and become livid when we refused to drop everything to answer his call.

Working with investors is not for the faint of heart.

Small Business Tip: Grow Relationships with Bankers. I approached a few banks in the early days for loans and lines of credit. Some were rude, and I'll never do business with them. But some took the time to review and show me where I needed to improve to get the financing I wanted. Even if it doesn't happen the first time you ask, stay in touch with people you meet at financial institutions. Send them updates and invite them to events. You never know when you'll be back in the market and in a better position to ask for money. I still use one of the banks I approached in those days as my primary bank. Since the initial request, I've opened several business and personal accounts with them. They send referrals, and I refer people to them. I can call on them anywhere and they will help me—like the time one of their commercial bankers set up my account to accept a certain type of payment while we were out of town on a business trip. That's good service! (Thank you, Sarah!)

A few years later, I went to that same local bank to sign loan documents for a business line of credit and a loan to buy equipment for a new venue. I was 30 years old and had already approached this banker three times for a loan or line of credit. By this time, the loan officer had known me for a few years. He'd seen me grow and build, and he developed confidence in me apart from my numbers. We had several accounts with money in the bank that he could see. His decisions to issue the line of credit and the loan were much easier to make because of the trust and confidence we'd created together.

Bills and Vendors

As your company grows, your accounts payable will change, too. The more money you earn, the more crap you have to pay for. Unfortunately, unless you're a magician and can make money without spending, prepare to deal with more bills, invoices, and vendors.

More online:

Early in my business ownership journey, I built relationships with a handful of our service providers. I referred them to others, maintained respect for their time and talents, and paid my bills on time. Whenever money got tight, I leaned on these vendors for help—and they came through. They extended payment terms, gave me discounts, and talked me off the ledge countless times. After I filed bankruptcy, they were the first to help me get back on my feet as I launched a new company. I attribute a large part of my success today to these generous providers.

One of these vendors is a local florist. She's a badass. I want to be her when I grow up. She has an amazing story of how she came to own her company. I can vent to her about client frustrations, money constraints, employee concerns, and anything that comes to mind—and she can do the same with me. She also covers my rear—often. If I need a last-minute event covered, or if I just need to make magic happen for a client, I lean on her. She sends clients my way and gives us preferred rates, which gives us a financial "win" when we pass them on to our clients and we can stretch an event budget. I know I can count on this friend, and I genuinely enjoy working with her. (*She's also "no nonsense," which, if you know me, you know I appreciate.*)

The first step to getting this kind of support? Align with vendors who provide a quality product or service, with fair and reliable pricing. Like anything else, when hiring vendors, make sure to research them and ensure they fit with your company. They become an extension of your team, but they don't work for you full-time, so you have to respect their schedule. If you don't get along with them, you probably won't work well together. You will rely on and spend a great amount of time and money with

Vendors You'll Need

Create a list of any vendor types you might need to work with for your business

More online:

them, so make sure it's worth it. Find out their payment terms. Do they match your accounts payable terms? Can you manage this service in-house, or is it necessary and better to outsource? Don't fear asking too many questions. You're a new, small start-up, and every penny counts. A few bad decisions with a vendor can literally bankrupt your company.

Small Business Tips: Vendor Research Can Save Your Business. I once hired a company to help us with marketing, website development, and social media management. I put something out on Facebook, and a friend connected me with a recommended company. Without doing much research, I met with the company and hired them a few weeks later. Looking back, I realize they asked for an absurd amount of money each month. Even worse—I didn't ask the right questions.

We agreed on a three-month contract, which would extend the rest of the year after the three months were assessed. After we signed the contract, I got passed off to a contractor in another state who didn't take time to learn and understand my business. I quickly realized I'd made a big mistake. I hadn't asked for references or examples of their work. I didn't really ask for anything. They made posts irrelevant to our events, they used a voice and tone that made us seem like a "low end" party planner creating princess parties out of our garage—and that's just the tip of the iceberg. I made a very expensive mistake that took me two years to recover from. So research vendors, ask tough questions, be thorough, and don't fear! Go with your gut, and always stay attuned to the work vendors do. You pay them, after all.

When it comes to bills, I want to stress the importance of forecasting. You'll find peaks and valleys with every company, so make sure you forecast upcoming expenses. If you have a big bill coming up, hold off on that extra magazine ad. Plan out your budget, stick to it, and always keep a little extra cash on hand for emergencies. You will *always have emergencies.*

Communication is a must. Let's be honest—sometimes a bill catches you by surprise. Maybe you over- or under-projected something, spent too much, lost a big account, or someone is late paying you. Money is tight. Welcome to the wonderful and stressful world of small-business ownership. Remember the key: *communication.* Stay in communication with your vendors and partners about your limitations. Don't be afraid to tell them you have a tight budget, you need to make payments, or you need to set up alternative options. They will understand (even if they don't say it) because they have probably been in a similar position at some point, too. Don't be surprised if they get annoyed or upset with you. After all, they are likely a small business as well, and they have to work through the same issues you do.

It took a while to get over my pride and be real with people when money got tight. As a new company, I wanted to be the "most successful" and the "most _____ [fill in the blank]." But I didn't actually have it all together, and pretending that I did pissed people off. Once I learned to communicate about where things stood, people felt more comfortable and tensions eased. I didn't avoid paying; I always pay my bills. But if the money wasn't there, there was nothing I could do about it.

After more than ten years in business, recovering from a bankruptcy *and* a global pandemic, we've earned respect and credit from our vendors. Year after year, as we increase our event production, grow revenue, and expand our footprint, our success has become *their* success, too. We have rental companies that turn other customers away, but will still give us deliveries even when they're fully booked. We have audio/video vendors that require payment in full before events... except *our* events, where they accept payment afterward. We have catering partners that pull out all the stops with two weeks' notice and make magic—if *we* are the ones asking for it. We've worked hard to build these relationships, and it shows through the trust our vendors place in us.

INVESTMENT:
WORK YOUR BUSINESS

05 | **NETWORKING**

PROMOTING YOURSELF AND YOUR BRAND

BUILD, CREATE, GROW

PARTNERSHIPS

Chapter Extras

Networking

Once you're established, seek industry-specific groups to join. These groups help you garner new business, build awareness, and grow your brand. We joined groups that connected us to other businesses: Business Networking International (BNI), Meeting Professionals International (MPI), Downtown Lexington Corporation, and Central Kentucky Wedding & Event Professionals (WEP). These industry-focused groups helped us grow our network of vendors we could refer to our clients. They also introduced us to city officials, CEOs and business owners of the region's biggest companies, and top decision-makers in our market. They called on us for event opportunities, and as we got better acquainted, they recommended me for board positions and connected me with opportunities I couldn't dream up.

Keep an eye out for niche groups. Can you find networking groups or associations related to your line of work, industry, product, or service? Do you work in a new market where it makes sense to join another Chamber? What about specific groups related to who you are as a person (young professional, minority, woman-owned, LGBTQ, etc.)?

As you grow, always keep positive relationships with the groups you join. You still need those connections. But over time, you should become more selective about new groups you join, and if you realize quickly that one isn't a good fit, don't waste time on it. Time is money, and some groups cost money. Money is money!

Promoting Yourself and Your Brand

During COVID, both of my businesses shut down completely. We couldn't operate events or venues, and I had plenty of time on my hands. So I hired my first business/personal coach. I joined a number of coaching groups and signed up for sessions and workshops. I enrolled virtually at Notre Dame and LSU to start a series of certifications and degrees. The first coach I hired told me I needed to do a better job of self-promotion. I hate to talk about myself, my accolades, things I do, or personal achievements. At first, it felt weird; I didn't want to come across as self-absorbed or overly confident. It took a lot of work, practice, and continual nudging from my coach to get in the habit of promoting myself on social media.

You won't get far if you fear promoting yourself and your brand. The problem is that no one else can or will do it—certainly not as authentically. You can do this strategically by working it into conversations casually, and carrying business cards everywhere you go. But you must work it into every conversation at least once, even if you only include it in your introduction.

You're an expert at what you do; it's not "bragging" to have confidence in your abilities. Before you sell to anyone else, you must sell yourself. If you lack confidence in yourself to deliver, why should anyone else trust you? To include the casual promotion, I mentioned the name of my company when introducing myself: "Hi! I'm Kaelyn Query Caldwell, Kentucky Event Company." My social media channels showcase a myriad of posts, some of which self-promote. I share awards I've received, articles where I've been published or profiled, work I've done —mixed in among my other posts. I word them purposefully to say, "Hey, look at this cool thing that happened!" or "I was honored to have received/been named/been included, etc.," instead of, "Look at me, look how great I am!"

Always jump on opportunities to attend events, set up a booth, or cross-promote. Don't miss this easy and sometimes free (or low cost) way to spread word about your company, product, or service.

Be the face of your brand. I sit on several boards across the state of Kentucky, and one national board for small business owners. I've gone from a "rookie" board member all the way up to board chair. I gain exposure through these positions, and my event company generally volunteers to lend a hand with fundraising events and efforts, earning additional recognition. This leads to awards like Entrepreneur of the Year (x2), Rookie of the Year, and 50 Under 50 (x2), a Small Business Advocate of the Year nomination, and more. Regardless of how many people work for you, at the end of the day—*you* built this. Don't shy away when people recognize or praise you. At first, it might feel weird, but let it soak in. Just stay humble and never let it go to your head.

Build, Create, Grow

When I started LexEffect Events, I had this grand idea of how we would grow and what we would achieve over the years. We'd produce events for others, work with non-profits, create our own series of events and shows, and make everything wonderful. I dove in headfirst. Instead of starting small and growing from there, I started by trying to have it all. We rolled out our new company, launched (literally) fourteen new concepts, produced events for corporate groups, social groups, non-profits, and wedding clients—all in the same breath. It was all too much.

Of course, we need to build our businesses—constantly, and consistently. If you aren't growing as a company, you won't survive. Without new avenues for revenue and exposure or new projects and partnerships, the business becomes stagnant. But as you build, keep in mind that there is such a thing as building "too much, too quickly." Keep the bigger picture in perspective, and build in a way that meets the needs of the company and supports the long term plan. Growth frequently requires changes, such as more employees, bigger offices, larger budgets, etc.

You can end up in an unfortunate position of "too big, too fast." This might sound contradictory, because without money, you have no business. But you need other important ingredients to achieve a successful company. Have you ever heard the saying, "You can't pour from an empty cup"? Mental health and wellbeing are just as important as sales, if not more. If you can't actually operate or work the business, sales don't really matter. As I became a more seasoned business owner, I realized I could make more money producing fewer events. *What?!* Don't get me wrong—I didn't *stop* working hard. Rather, I prioritized vetting clients to ensure our priorities aligned, I adjusted our pricing to match the level of service, work, and experience we had, and we stopped taking new clients for their own sake. I also got better at managing boundaries, my schedule, and my "free" time—which led to greater happiness. I became nicer to my clients and team—what a concept!

In hindsight, the rate at which LexEffect grew is one of my biggest frustrations and regrets. Instead of ensuring we were prepared, I charged ahead full-throttle. Some concepts that could have been successful failed instead. We lost employees who would have been great, and we rejected the stability small startups desperately need. Instead of focusing on the clients we had, I went into sales mode and closed every deal I could. I focused on the bottom line—making payroll. I failed to focus on things I could control (like expenses), and assumed I could solve our problems by selling more events. The problem with this approach was that we lacked capacity to execute more events—we had no structure in place to fulfill them. I could have avoided a ton of issues, financial or otherwise, if I'd focused on operating the business instead of making more sales. There's a fine line between healthy growth, versus growth for its own sake.

Partnerships

There are two kinds of "partners"—formal partnerships (like a business partner) and a "symbiote" (two LLCs who help one another). I attempted business partners... once. A few years ago, I produced a music festival (which I normally self-funded) with two partners. LexEffect kept growing, and became harder to sustain with my own money. Contrary to what some people think, large festivals and events take several years to actually turn a profit. So, after the 2016 festival, we were short about $45,000 in expenses. You can't get a loan for a business loss like this; banks don't cover things with 100% risk. So I had to find a private option.

Enter my two business "partners." They covered the loss for 50% equity in the company (This festival was a stand-alone LLC). Unfortunately, I moved too fast and didn't cover my bases. The operating agreement wasn't fully fleshed out. The partners *only* covered the loss and nothing additional, and we had no "tie breaker" in place if we had a future disagreement, since we had 50/50 ownership. They made big promises, like help for producing the event,

More online:

connections, and financial contributions. We had *big* plans to grow the festival, and I felt confident and comfortable moving ahead with them on my side.

Fast forward to summer 2017—we doubled our event budget under their guidance, and pushed full-steam ahead on producing the festival again. But the help they promised never materialized. In fact, it was quite the opposite—they did everything they could to hinder the production. We knew two months prior that we would likely be short on expenses for the event. They agreed to cover the loss (as part of our five-year plan to grow the festival). They also told me to go to the vendors, leverage my relationships, and get deferred payments (post-festival instead of pre-festival). The festival came and went, and sure enough, we took a loss. The partners approved the checks for the vendors (part of our operating agreement), but as I left the bank to deliver the payments, I got a call to inform me that the checks were voided and the money removed from the account. These two guys refused to pay, blocked me from filing bankruptcy for the company (which resulted in a bankruptcy for another company), and left me holding the bag. They took my plans, my sponsors, and the money, and they started a new festival.

I haven't had business partners since.

Now, *businesses* that you partner with are a different story. We work with a wholesale florist, the one I mentioned previously, and she is invaluable to our company. Not only does she price her products fairly, but she is a great partner. She lets me vent about frustrations with clients or employees, and she shares her frustrations too. She bails me out when we get last-minute client requests or a client changes their mind. She makes magic happen without charging an arm and a leg. She simply makes us look good. More times than I can count, she's stepped in to help when other vendors fell short. At times, she's literally saved an entire event while making us look like superheroes because of the short notice.

Building strong partnerships will prove to be one of the best moves you can make in business. Unless you have significant startup capital, you'll have a tight budget in the early years. You won't have disposable income for photography, videography, fancy collateral, or marketing. Partnerships work around this obstacle by trading products and services with other small businesses. Partnerships with vendors are equally critical because you can exchange favors like on-account payment and last-minute requests. Good partners care for your clients when you refer them, and that makes *you* look good.

More online:

More online:

Interns are another form of partnership: you gain free or low-cost labor to help with small tasks, odd jobs, and overall business functions. Partner with local colleges, career centers, and other employee placement organizations to find interns. You're responsible for making the internship worthwhile, especially if it's unpaid. Intern placement organizations will advise you of rules and regulations on the number of hours interns can work and what types of jobs they can do. Internships offer a great way to find out whether or not someone makes a good potential fit as an employee for your company (and for them to decide if your industry is right for them).

We had a robust internship program at LexEffect, and we required participation from everyone who worked for us. We offered three internship terms—Spring, Summer, and Fall—and we normally had around ten interns per term. Some folks accepted purely for experience and class credit, but others came because they wanted a job. This gave us a ninety-day period to learn about a potential employee and determine if they fit with the team and the company. In exchange, it gave interns an inside look at our values and culture, the way we operated, and whether we made a good match for them.

Paid or unpaid, internship programs take work to set up and maintain. You have to follow rules for an internship or unpaid position. Similar to contractors, be careful with how much you involve them. We spent hours each week teaching interns how to do certain tasks. When you start out and can't afford to hire employees, interns may be your best solution. A well-trained intern can function as a great asset—and become dedicated, long-term employees. We've had several interns-turned-employees throughout our history. Even long after they leave, we can still call on them to jump in and help.

INVESTMENT:
MOTIVATION

06 | **MOTIVATING YOURSELF**
INSPIRATION
YOU TIME
BALANCING

Chapter Extras

I've said it before, but I'll say it again for the people in the back: Business ownership is not for the faint of heart. It's exhausting and pushes you to the brink—and then back again. You can easily hit burnout by losing motivation—the "why"—of your business and mission. You can drown quickly in payroll, sales, inventory, and expenses, so you *must* stay motivated. But don't be fooled. There are "good" (positive) motivators and also "bad" (negative) motivators.

"Yes" People and "No" People

In my third year of business as LexEffect Events, I wrapped our biggest event of the year. It was $45,000 in the hole.

You have no idea what stress is until you have payroll, a mountain of outstanding bills, and an unexpected loss of $45,000. I had already written checks for the event that weekend—without cash in hand to cover them. (This is a big no-no. Do *not* do this.)

Three days later, I had a new partner who covered the loss. I made a blind ask, and I couldn't believe a partnership came through. One month later, we missed another event mark and I had to round up another $24,000. The year before, both of these events had either broken even or earned a net profit... but this year, neither came close.

Small business is a rollercoaster ride - there are issues that arise that you might expect, such as cash flow issues or employee drama - but then you get blindsided with an issue you never saw coming, like business partners who go out of their way to put you out of business. You can't take it on lightly, and it will break you down and beat you up like you've never experienced.

To survive and stay motivated, you need two kinds of people: YES people and NO people.

YES

You'll come across huge highs in business that make it all worthwhile—and then you get smacked in the back of the head with a 2x4, bringing you back to reality. To avoid losing your mind, you need a YES person. This person needs to be your biggest fan, your cheerleader, someone with a level head who isn't too cheesy—but always there to help you up when you get knocked down. They encourage and remind you of your mission. They tell you, "YES, you can!" You can … you will … and you must. It could be the same pep talk every time, but you will need it —and it feels new every time you hear it. You won't get through the early years without a YES person.

My YES person was my mother. Until the day she passed, I could call her any time of day and she'd pick up on the third ring. You've never met a bigger cheerleader for my business ventures. She was *always* on Team Kaelyn, and would hype me up no matter the circumstances. Even if we were annoyed with each other about another topic, she was *on it* if I called her about business. She rarely knew anything about the client, the business, or the industry—but she was *in* to give me encouragement I needed.

A few rules for the YES person:

- They cannot also be your NO person—ever! These must be two separate people. Your YES person has only one job.

- Your YES person is not there to give you advice. They are there to build you up and remind you why you do what you do. They don't reason, or play devil's advocate. This person helps you keep pushing toward your goals and desires.

NO

While you need someone to build you up, you also need a boldly realistic voice: the NO person. This is the person you go to for advice and feedback, and who plays devil's advocate. They help you think strategically, and fearlessly tell you, "NO."

> *"No, this idea won't work!"*
>
> *"No, you shouldn't take on another project!"*
>
> *"No, you aren't looking at this correctly!"*

Who Are Your "Yes" People?

More online:

Who Are Your "No" People?

Now, sometimes your NO person might say "Yes" to something you discuss. That's fine, but you still need them to help you look at your ideas from different angles. The NO person helps you make better decisions and learn when to say "No" for yourself. Jay, my SBDC advisor, was my first NO person. He stayed respectful and polite, but on the right occasions, he firmly said "No." He showed me the other side, vetted the details, and looked at situations through lenses that were foreign to me. As I outgrew SBDC services, my dad became my second NO person. My siblings would agree – my dad more quickly says "No" than "Yes." He didn't understand my business or the industry, which gave him pause anytime I had a new idea. He gave a thumbs down to several ideas I threw at him. His negativity annoyed me. I'd never admit it to him (*not even today, so ssshhh, don't read this aloud to him*), but his hesitation proved right. (*But don't tell him I said that.*)

A few rules for the NO person:

- This person cannot ever be your YES person. The NO person is for advice, not a pep talk.

- Your NO person must not be an advisor or mentor who sits on your advisory/mentor board. It must be an individual you refer to only for these types of questions. Don't look for someone who vehemently dislikes you, or your company or your industry. You want someone who questions the ideas, provides a different perspective, asks tough questions, and always wants more answers. This person should not have a conflict of interest in your company, i.e. an investor or lender.

You won't always take the advice of your YES person or your NO person. They're not substitute decision-makers. You need them to force yourself to think twice before making a big move.

Motivating Yourself

List Your Personal Goals Here:

More online:

T he days will come when you've put in 200% effort, 100+ hours a week, and you're out of energy. When you feel like you can't do anything right, and you're ready to give up. When you feel *exhausted*, you must dig deep to recover your motivation.

I'm a big fan of setting goals. At the beginning of each year, I create several goals: personal, business, financial, and health goals. I write them down in my planner and post them on the wall in my office. I track them throughout the year, and I check to see how I'm stacking up. Midway through the year, I deep dive into where things stand, and I look at how I can improve or change to achieve my goals by the end of the year. Then, at year's end, I post results for *all* my goals on Linkedin—to be transparent and accountable to myself and to encourage other small business owners, so they can see it's not always sunshine and rainbows. If I don't define what I plan to strive for, how will I know if I achieve anything? If I don't set a goal and track it, how will I know if I grow or not?

Get started thinking about goals. A worksheet is provided at the end of this chapter.

Inspiration

A few years ago, I went to work for an event production company based in California. I'd lost inspiration for self-employment. I had grown weary from the overflow of COVID for the event industry and the difficulty of staging events after the pandemic. We did double the events for half the pay, with a quarter of the staff. I was tired of being in charge and working seven days a week. We produced about two hundred events a year, and I was burned out. I'd lost my "why," and I thought working for someone else might help reignite that passion. I could get back to the creative outlet of planning and producing events and get away from payroll, taxes, and business development meetings.

As much as you need motivation, you also need inspiration. They are not the same things. *Motivation* is the reason behind your action, whereas *inspiration* is the mental or emotional push or pull from the results of your efforts. I get inspired every time we produce a large event. When I'm on the show floor and the music plays and people cheer—it inspires me to create.

I'm motivated to build this business because I enjoy the lifestyle it affords me and the freedom and flexibility to create. I'm motivated by the outlets I've been given to continue to explore and learn and teach—all of which I'd lose if I worked for someone else. But I get inspired by the "peak" moments of events, even by events other people produce. I feel inspired when I learn, grow, and create a legacy for my family. I print out and save inspirational quotes that speak to me, and I hang them on the wall in front of my desk. They help me keep perspective, stay

List Your Business Goals Here:

focused, and remember my "why" when I feel down.

It never fails: when I need a pick-me-up, I look up from my desk and see the quotes on the wall. My outlook shifts immediately and I can keep going. Inspiration for my business came from planning and designing successful events. When our company got bigger, I moved out of the event planning role and into a development/management position. I'm good at management, and I know I made the right move, but occasionally I take on an event planning role to breathe life back into my passion for the industry.

I get inspired by how our events benefit their communities. I serve on several non-profit boards and charity event planning committees, and donate heavily to the non-profit community through my companies. I made this my mission from the beginning, and it's a big part of what inspires me every day. The impact we make for non-profits through their fundraising events amazes me.

Eventually, the California company I worked for gave notice that it would have to furlough its entire staff indefinitely. I felt crushed. I'd sold my venus company and had nearly closed out my events company. I'd put all my eggs in this one basket, only to find out the basket had a hole in it. Back to the drawing board! I had to reinvent myself and what I would do—*again*. I looked for other jobs, but nothing sparked joy like events did. I needed to recreate that feeling. The good news was that this time, I could do it with all the knowledge I learned the hard way the first time around. I could create a better version of what I originally set out to do, and I could find my passion again. I decided:

- I would *not* work 100-hour weeks again and miss out on all of life.

- I would *not* settle for events and clients that didn't fit with our mission, our schedule, or our goals.

- I would *not* fear saying "no" to opportunities or requests that overloaded my calendar.

- I would protect my time and my boundaries, and I would set a better work schedule.

- I would ensure that I set up my finances in a much better format than the first time around.

- I would charge what I deserved, based on my skills, experience, connections, and my team, instead of charging what I thought the client might be OK with paying. And if that meant I didn't get the gig, I *would* be OK with that.

I'd paid several big prices to feel this degree of certainty and confidence. In my opinion, all great business owners need to mature to the point that they refuse to compromise on their core priorities. For me, I would never again do business if I had to sacrifice "me time," or live life without balance.

More online:

You Time

In the early days, I felt driven to work all the time. I was a small startup, and had to do everything. Plus, according to my family's narrative, successful people worked "all day, every day." I spread myself too thin, which meant I had to work nonstop to keep up. It left me no time for myself or activities I enjoyed outside of business. But I loved what I did for work—so that should have been enough, right?

Business demands endless work. It's stressful and time consuming, but guess what? The human spirit needs rest and replenishing. You shouldn't feel guilty about this; in fact, *schedule it*. What are you passionate about, aside from work? What makes you happier than anything else? What relaxes you? What makes stress fade away? Find those things, and do them often. I still struggle to take time away, go on vacations, or reserve time for myself. I feel guilty, as though I'm letting clients down, or I might miss out on something big or important. My clients take vacations and never apologize for it—so why do I feel guilty about taking time to recharge?

Get Away. Whether you take a weekend away or have a staycation at home cleaning out the closet – you need to get away, turn off the computer, and shut your "work brain" off. I had no money in the beginning, so going on trips was out of the question. But sometimes I needed a weekend or a day without an agenda or a meeting. A pause where I could sleep in, clean up the house, do laundry, or read a book. I just needed time away from the hustle.

Relax. Occasionally, when I come home from work, or have a moment to put up my feet, I grab some red wine and watch *Law & Order*. You need to find something that makes you relax. Do you enjoy yoga? Cooking a meal? Gardening? Whatever helps you de-stress, make sure to do it often. You'll always have plenty of hard work, early mornings, late nights, and putting in the extra effort—but learn to switch it off. If you don't take time away from work, you won't be your best when you need to switch on.

Family and Friends. Just as you make time for yourself, make time for family and friends. Entrepreneurship takes you down a hard and lonely road, and it forces you to put other parts of your life on hold. When you get a chance, touch base with those relationships and let them know you still exist.

More online:

The old adage says, "No matter where you go, there you are." If you go through something in your personal life, it carries over into work. And if you have stress at work, that follows you home. You have to make a conscious decision every time to turn off "work" and focus on your family and friends. It takes practice, and if you're like me, it will take a lot of hard work to retrain your brain to put a pause on work tasks.

If you don't learn this skill, you'll jeopardize the quality of your relationships. I have to work hard at this every day. When my mother passed away, this became even more important. I realized how quickly life can change and how truly unimportant that "one quick, last email" really is. I'm not saying blow past deadlines or ignore your work responsibilities. But when you are on "family time," engage in family time. Be where your feet are, as my friend Vitale always says.

Balancing

Entrepreneurship is a juggling act: work tasks, employees, payroll, marketing, clients, accounts payable, new systems, vendors, invoices, accounts receivable, office management, and so forth. What motivates you to keep the balancing act going?

Many people think that starting your own company means an abundance of free time and tons of money. It's not true, at least initially. Yes, you do get to make your own schedule, but the schedule includes being the first one in and the last one out. It means working when no one else does, and no one else will. It's putting in more than one hundred hours a week without a paycheck for three years, while your employees work 40-60 hours a week, making $60,000+ a year with benefits and vacation days. Did I mention you don't have much money? I put every penny I had into starting my business. Without significant startup capital, there wasn't much to go around. I was so committed to making my company succeed that I sacrificed my own paycheck for the first three years to pay my employees a good salary, introduce new projects, and make it through slow months.

Make sure you can balance everything it takes to start a business, and don't fall for an illusion of ample free-time or money. I'll paraphrase one of my mentors : Employees serve one person—their direct supervisor at the place where they work. Entrepreneurs serve multiple people—customers, employees, shareholders, vendors, their community, and so on. If you want free time and easy money, apply for a 9a-5p job, and leave it at that. Entrepreneurship means you work your tail off and make yourself valuable to hundreds of people. If you only want leisure time and cash, you'll be disappointed. Money and free time can give you a long-term motivator, but you can only really get them by giving them up in the first place. The day may come when you have served others so well that the business runs without you and you still get paid. Forget about the mimosas and the beachfront condo —they're not coming in the early years of your entrepreneurship journey… Sorry to be the one to break it to you.

What Stands Out For You:

More online:

INITIATIVE:
GROWTH

07 | **TAKING A STEP BACK**
ACCEPTING AND **EMBRACING CHANGE**
EVALUATING AND **ADJUSTING**
FINANCIALS AND **BUDGETS**
KNOWING WHEN TO **WALK AWAY**

Chapter Extras

Taking a Step Back

If I'd stepped back and reviewed LexEffect Events' financial snapshot, I would have closed the doors much sooner. That investor "agreement" kept us underwater, overextending our capabilities. Our payroll-heavy budget limited us, we charged too little for our services, and we served clients we should have declined… just to stay afloat.

It's important to take a step back and put on your "objectivity" glasses. As one of my former partners put it, take a 40,000-foot view of your business. Are you profitable, or on track to be? Are you still working towards your plan and meeting your goals? Do you need to adjust? Unless you review, you can't ensure you're succeeding. I also recommend having someone else examine it with you to see the full picture.

You must also take a step back to look at the picture *outside* of your business. How much of your life have you given up? Is it still worth it? Do you still believe in it? When I started my business in 2013, I moved back home with my parents and rented my own house to a tenant. I reduced my bills and my spending, and I avoided trips and outings. By my fourth year of business, I had creditors calling me hourly. I owed more money than I could fathom paying off, had very few friends, and a non-existent love life. My work relationships were drowning, and I felt like I had wasted years building a business that would end up failing anyway. I needed to step back, reassess, re-position, and renew my passion for the endeavor I had started.

What followed was a long, emotionally intricate process to figure it out on my own. I unplugged completely from the business, went to the woods (my happy place), and sat alone with my thoughts and a journal.

Taking a step back looks different for each of us. It also depends on the phase of your business (first year versus tenth year). Sometimes the "step back" gets forced on us, in the way of a medical issue, loss of a loved one, or some other massive disruption. And sometimes, you need others' help to reevaluate. Sometimes you need a second (or third) set of eyes to catch things you might miss —or won't let yourself see.

Accepting and Embracing Change

In 2015, we began consulting for event venues. As planners who worked in every venue in the area, we knew what venues needed and didn't need. We knew which venues we loved working in, and why. We knew what clients liked. With my catering background, I also knew their needs from a catering and logistics standpoint. This led us to consult for several big venues in central Kentucky, which led to venue branding and operations. In turn, that led to managing event venues and, eventually, owning our own.

With each new endeavor, we learned valuable lessons, and grew in understanding our capabilities and passions. We improved how we operated venues, as well as how much we charged. Some of these lessons cost us more money than we liked, and some resulted in cutting ties or threats of lawsuits. Some took a lot of blood, sweat, and tears. Everyone has good intentions for their policies and procedures, but those don't always work out the way you hope. You must accept and embrace the change, and then you must adapt with it. Successful business leaders survive and thrive because they know how to handle change. They see a need, a new technology, a trend—and they jump on it. You must do the same.

Not long ago, we opened the first venue we'd created fully on our own. Start to finish, we created the venue concept, brand, operations structure, opened the doors, and then managed the property. We earned a monthly management fee and shared revenue from every event we booked. The venue hosted public concerts and ticketed events as well as private events like weddings.

At the outset, we didn't control the money; the owners did. So all client payments, ticket sales, bar sales—every penny went to and through the owners. Eventually, they stopped taking care of venue-related needs (like toilet paper and furniture). They stopped paying for the radio ads they committed to buy, and they began turning down revenue opportunities they didn't like. We had to cover some expenses to keep operations going and fight tooth-and-nail to get reimbursed. They insisted on "approving" each event, which meant that we didn't make money for our efforts. Eventually, we parted ways, but we learned valuable (expensive) lessons. From then on, we never let anyone else control the money. We required payment up front, controlled the books internally, and paid our partners. Never again would we fight for payment for doing our job. Never again would we cover operating expenses for a business we didn't own.

Evaluating and Adjusting

Be prepared to evaluate and adjust the business' direction along the way—many times. You will plateau and find that what previously worked … no longer fits. Some concepts lose relevance, and if you don't adjust your business model, you have a good chance of it dying in its tracks.

LexEffect once produced charity events for nonprofits, free of charge. Does that sound crazy? Yep! Everyone I knew told me it wouldn't work, but I was determined to do it anyway.

For one, I was the only employee; I had no other employees or overhead. To me, a free event equaled another day's work. I produced over 40 free events that year. I had plenty of other paying events, so money was not (entirely) a problem. I considered these free events as additional chances to get my name out there. They came with terms: the non-profit had to list my company as a sponsor or partner of the event. If they felt I did a good job, I urged them to write a recommendation. In exchange, I assisted them in producing and managing the event. I taught them how to pitch sponsors and partners. I created sponsor collateral for them, and gave them the contact information of potential sponsors or donors.

Through these events, I created a group of advocates for the LexEffect brand. I took each event seriously and put forth 110% in everything I did. It wasn't long before I'd worked with almost every non-profit in town. I gained a full portfolio and resume of clients I'd worked with, and built an impeccable track record of funds raised based on our plans.

Now, who do you think attends charity events? If you guessed "weatlhy people who run companies, whose kids are getting married, and who work on future events that might need our help," you're correct. Several of these nonprofits hired us for more robust (paid) help on future projects. They saw the benefit and worked our fee into their budget. And they justified it with their boards of directors after proof-of-concept. If you perform well with small things, people will trust you with bigger things.

This worked for me for my first year in business because I needed to prove myself. After year one, I'd hired an employee with benefits, the overhead became more substantial, and I couldn't spend as much time on free events. The original purpose of free charity events was to help organizations continue their work. But at the end of the day, I needed to earn income. I had to adjust the business model to support the charity efforts while still earning enough to support the company's financial needs.

So I started our Community Involvement program, which offers assistance to non-profit organizations in Central Kentucky. We provide monetary donations, event support, consulting—a variety of resources available through an application process. This allows us to maintain commitment to the community while not overextending ourselves with free events. I felt serious enough about our "why" to keep it as part of our company mission, but I had to adjust by figuring out how to make it work financially.

Financials and Budgets

H ere's another valuable lesson that took three years in business to learn. In our third year, we had a cash flow problem. In the event industry, you pay for everything up front. Expenses came larger and faster than revenue. When you add in a few of my bad business deals, the bottom line (literally) was that we were behind, by a country mile.

Our biggest problem was a lack of budgets or proper financial statements. Our accounts payable system was a joke. We had no accounts receivable process. Our P&L report might as well have been written on toilet paper. We had no plan or method for looking back to see where we'd improved, or failed to improve. Moreover, because we lacked a good grasp on our finances, we misread serious revenue and expense issues within our team. I didn't realize how much money we regularly "gave away." We offered discounts of up to 50% —for no reason. We gave quotes for services without getting actual prices from vendors, and when the final bill came due, we had to cover the difference in cost. Our team had no direction or management from a financial standpoint, and we suffered because of it.

Don't get me wrong: We had good intentions and a desirable offer. But to grow and improve, you need these two factors:

1. A rock-solid list of what you've done and where you stand financially. How much have you earned, what recurring sources of revenue do you have, and what accounts payable are expected.

2. A fleshed out roadmap and plan for where you are going, with goals and expectations. This includes new markets are you trying to tap, new clients you're trying to land, and new sources of revenue you plan to acquire.

For the first time in the history of LexEffect, I figured those two needs out. When I did, it felt like removing a 200-pound weight from my shoulders. We went through a lengthy process to get our accounting and bookkeeping corrected. The following year, we created an excellent, thorough plan that covered expenses, repaid debts, forecast revenue, and made clear what we could/could not afford. At last, we had a solid budget for each event instead of a quick budget with lots of holes. We created an approved monthly budget for marketing with advance awareness of leaner months. I knew how many employees I could add and how many events or dates we needed to make things work. This took three people working together, for more than 80 hours over two weeks, nonstop, and more than 20 changes between the first and final versions.

Flesh out your budget at the beginning. It saves money and time, and it will help you make better decisions. Here's a quick list of things you need to make your roadmap:

- All debts, by name and amount

- All assumed recurring revenues (renewals, recurring clients, etc.)
- All projected revenues (growth, added clients, etc.—be conservative)
- All expenses, by name and amount
- Miscellaneous expenses, because you'll definitely forget something

Once you make these lists, walk away for a day or two and think on it. Input all this data into a spreadsheet … and then walk away for a day or two and think about it again (I say this twice because taking space to reassess with a new headspace is always important, especially when talking about money and finances). Repeat this until you get it fleshed out, adjusting for areas where expenses are high and revenues low.

If you've been in business for a while, you should have most of this in your accounting system already, which makes the process easier. You should have a clear picture of how you've grown, and what growth you might expect in the future. Or, you might see areas in your business with potential for growth.

More online

Knowing When to Walk Away

Do you recall the story of the music festival where we fell short on expenses and brought on those two partners to help cover the losses? They doubled our budget to help grow the show, even though the market was down across the country. In general, music festivals were selling poorly at the time. We knew in advance that we would lose money, but my partners assured me we'd be okay. We'd take the loss, but it was a long game play; we had a five-year plan. They told me to ask for deferred payments, payment plans, and favors. I had good relationships with these folks, and they all agreed.

When the event ended, I went to get checks for the final payments post-event, and the bank told me the money was gone from the account. My partners had blocked use of the funds; the festival was now insolvent. These same two partners blocked me from filing bankruptcy for the festival company - and based on our operating agreement, I couldn't file for it without their consent. So, when some of the creditors from the festival wanted their money, and couldn't get it from the festival company … they instead came after LexEffect for the money.

My attorney at the time advised me to file bankruptcy and move on. It would be a long road to fight those two partners, and he wasn't willing to help me. So I found a new attorney - who also told me to file bankruptcy, but added that if I decided to fight, she would help me. Before we could fight my business partners, we had to deal with other lawsuits knocking at the door. One band in particular sued us for the balance owed from the festival. Despite legal proof showing the festival company was named on the contract and owed them money, they pursued my company anyway. (Fun fact: if you don't address the "venue" clause in a contract, you can be sued in California. Which means you must hire a California attorney to represent your Kentucky attorney. Which means TWO hourly fees.)

We offered settlements, which the band declined. We told them we didn't have the money they were after, and we didn't owe it to them. For the next two years, everything I earned went to cover payroll and legal fees. Every time the phone rang, I thought I would vomit. I stopped answering calls where I didn't recognize the number, because I expected another lawsuit. I hid from everyone. I became stressed, anxious, and on

More online:

edge nonstop. My business and my personal life suffered. I was miserable.

But I refused to file bankruptcy. I had built LexEffect from scratch, and put in all the effort to make it work: my life, blood, sweat, and tears. I'd given up EVERYTHING for this company, and I wouldn't walk away with nothing to show for it. It was my "kid," my identity - and what would I be without it? I fought and fought until I had nothing left. I became physically ill and worked myself into the hospital, twice.

Finally, after one last settlement attempt, I filed for bankruptcy for LexEffect Events. It was 10:00 AM. I shotgunned a beer after the call with my attorney - and it felt like 1000 pounds lifted from my shoulders. Then I called every client, vendor, and partner so I could tell them the news, from my own mouth, instead of them hearing it from the court or through the grapevine. I wish I'd filed two years earlier - but if I'd done that, I might not have learned everything I know now. I wouldn't have the thick skin I have today.

This goes for bankruptcy, as well as ordinary business and business deals. Sometimes you have to know when to walk away. I can't tell you how many times I stayed in a bad deal for some stupid reason. Sometimes things just don't work out, and part of being a good entrepreneur is knowing when to walk away.

Bad deals last longer than contracts. Sometimes they take years to level out, and sometimes, no matter how hard you try or how much work you put in, they just don't work out.

It's OK. It's scary, but it's OK.

I was scared to file bankruptcy. I feared for my reputation, livelihood, and identity. But I filed, went through the motions of bankruptcy, and I'm happy to say … I didn't die. I went to court, and some creditors came and asked for money. I was honest with my clients. None of them yelled at me, or laughed, or really cared. Eventually I started a new business called Lexington Event Company. I'm still here.

Don't get me wrong - avoid bankruptcy like the plague, unless you have no alternative. It's not cheap, and it's not fun. But it's not the end of all things.

More online:

INITIATIVE:
EMPLOYEES

Chapter Extras

Hiring

You see your business growing and making money, but you feel overwhelmed with the workload and need extra help. What's next? Do you consider hiring?

There's a fine line between the *need* to hire and the *ability* to do it. As the saying goes, "Which comes first? The chicken, or the egg?" In our case, we needed enough events to overwhelm us, so that we couldn't afford *not* to hire someone. At the same time, the worst thing you can do is hire too many people, or hire them too soon. Nothing is as stressful as asking employees to do work you normally do yourself. I recommend providing your service by yourself for as long as you can. But if you want to scale and grow, at some point you'll need help.

Full Time, Part time, Contract

When you get ready to hire, you need a crash course in human resources (HR). Your local Small Business Development Center can help. You need to know the difference between full-time/part-time (W-2) and contract (1099) employees. Each kind has certain requirements, restrictions, and tax procedures. Before you hire, you must know *exactly* what it will cost to hire someone for the role. For sales staff especially, you must be able to project that the revenue they bring will cover their costs—and then some.

More online: If you're hiring an employee in a non-sales position, the relief they offer must open up lanes to acquire more revenue. When you hire them, your sales team should gain more time and space to sell. Employees cost more than mere salary or hourly pay! You also pay taxes, matching contributions, benefits, vacation time, sick time, holidays, and incentives. Employees require management and training, and sometimes they need therapy and parenting. Here is a general breakdown of the three employee types. Be sure to check them against your local city and state laws and regulations.

Full-Time employees typically work a full-time schedule as outlined by their employers. Full-time employees normally receive benefits, bonuses, and/or other perks not provided for part-time and contract employees. These might include health and dental coverage, paid vacation days, and so forth. Full-time could mean salary or hourly, but normally averages from 32-60 hours per week. Some full-time employees are exempt from overtime, some are not. You can dictate schedule, business hours, equipment, attire, and more to a full-time employee.

Part-Time employees typically work 20-32 hours or less per week, almost always on an hourly pay basis. Part-time work can be seasonal or year-round, and in some cases, they can receive perks and benefits. Similar to full-time employees, you can control part-time employees a bit more when it comes to schedule, attire, equipment, work hours/location, and more.

Contract Labor includes any individual who works on a project or task basis; you only pay them for that specific work. We hire contract labor staff for some of our bigger events. They do not work enough with us on a weekly basis to qualify as a part-time or full-time employee. We pay them a flat rate for each event based on the agreement. Another great example would be a freelance graphic designer; you pay them a rate per design piece, and they send you an invoice. They don't have a desk at your office or work specific hours.

We often hire contractors seasonally. I don't require them to work specific hours, nor do I provide uniforms or company equipment for them. Rules for contractors are set by federal and state governments, and they are non-negotiable. You don't pay taxes on contract labor, and you don't match retirement contributions. On the downside (sometimes), contractors are free to go work elsewhere as well. They aren't always as available as other hired employees.

Dealing with Employees

It would be nice if hiring employees led to rainbows and sunshine until the end of time... but that doesn't always happen. It will probably take you three to four hires to find a rockstar. And if there's a downside to rockstars, it's this: someone else (like a competitor) meets them, also thinks they are a rockstar, and lures them away with greater reward for their efforts. In the meantime, you get to deal with the two to three shit employees on the rockstar's left and right. I could write another book about the nonsense I've dealt with from employees. If you run a company that needs staff, prepare yourself for a rollercoaster of crazy managing people. We once hired an employee who seemed fantastic during the interview phase. She was assertive in trying to connect about the job, she worked her way through four different connections she had to me, and she asked each of them to reach out to me directly about interviewing her for the job. I blew her off three times, and she still periodically came back to check about the position. We finally interviewed her, and before we even sent her the official offer, she posted on Linkedin she had accepted the position. Yikes!

During her first few months, we noticed she was *great* with people. This was uncommon among twenty-somethings with no event experience. She had the "it" factor when she communicated. She had a firm handshake, she'd look you in the eye, she had a gregarious personality, and communicated well with clients. But at everything else ... she failed.

During on-site events, we had to micro-manage her tasks. Her administrative work looked like a mess. She never followed through, had trouble following directions, and created more work for me than she was worth. Inevitably, this led to several dropped balls that resulted in frustrated clients. After four months, we had to part ways.

Another time, I hired someone who had a great resumé for sales. We needed a dedicated sales manager to backfill my workload. His sole job was to bring in leads and tee up the conversation so I could close. But resumés are hard to prove. This person either had zero real experience, or somehow forgot everything he'd learned when he came to work with us. He quickly caused rifts with other team members, and it wasn't long before everyone hated him. For a small company with an open-office concept, this caused a bad situation. We realized he wasn't actually selling anything. He didn't create new connections, build relationships, or generate business for the company. I had to decide between him and the rest of the team. I'll let you guess which one I chose.

Then there was the intern who constantly missed work. She sent me a text at 2:00 AM on a Saturday telling me her grandmother had passed and she had to skip an event that was two weekends away, so she could attend the funeral. It seemed a little odd that she decided this at 2:00 AM on a Saturday—but I didn't want to assume. Reality came back to bite, though. A week later, I told her I needed her to bring something from her grandmother's funeral so I could record the absence with her school. She received class credit for the internship, and their protocol was to document absences with some kind of evidence. She seemed surprised, but she agreed.

The following week she showed up with a "program" from the funeral. It resembled an art project from my three-year-old son's preschool class. You know, the ones with the scissors with the jagged edges.

This wasn't my first rodeo. I knew the internet would most likely have a record of the obituary, so I typed in the first few sentences from the program. I learned the grandmother in this program had actually died three days *after* the intern told me she needed to attend her funeral—and also, she wasn't really her grandmother! I called her into the office and asked her for the truth. She doubled down, until I showed her the original obituary from the internet. Needless to say, I immediately fired her, which also resulted in a zero for the course and her having to retake her entire college class.

Some employees really suck. Take the guy who thinks he works hard… when in reality, he shows up at 12pm, leaves at two, and smells like the bar from the night before. Or how about the girl who never pays attention and makes costly mistakes, but who gives you attitude because she's "too good" for certain tasks? Employees who regularly disregard your direction and guidance and then have the nerve to look confused

More online:

while they're being written up. Employees whose personal lives constantly interfere with the business, and when you object as the owner… they blame you! Employees who believe you owe them something, even though you pay them to be there. The list goes on.

I'll share my top tips, taken from all my mistakes with employees… rockstars and shitheads alike:

1. Set Expectations – When you hire someone, set the expectations for the job up front. Make sure you clearly express what you expect them to accomplish, how you view their role in the company, and how you expect the office to run. Talk about it, put it in writing, and review it often. No matter how clear you think you are… assume you always have more to explain, over and over again (because you do). I recommend creating an employee handbook. Write all of your expectations and standard instructions down where employees can reference it and easily access it. You can also use it to make company-wide updates and inform everyone of changes and developments. If you don't set clear expectations, don't expect employees to follow the rules.

2. Three-Strike Policy – From the beginning, enforce a three-strike policy (or whatever you are comfortable with), and stick to it. You need a system to handle issues fairly while preventing people from walking all over you. Some boundaries are **hard** (such as theft, harassment, or assault), while others are **soft** (negligence or occasional tardiness). Decide on those hard and soft boundaries, make them clear to everyone, and stick to them.

3. Stay Consistent – Similar to the Three-Strike Policy, be fair and consistent. If you play favorites, you'll lose credibility. Sometimes the rockstars slip, too, but you can't let slide for them what you would reprimand in someone else. My employees may have said I was "tough," but none of them said I was unfair. I didn't care if an employee was my roommate, my sibling, or my best friend— everyone got the same treatment.

4. Don't Hire Friends or Family – Don't do it. This is a really bad idea. We'll get into this more later, but for now… just… don't.

5. Write-Ups – Keep written records of everything, and make sure it's printed and signed. Document all reprimands and reviews (create a template in advance), and keep them in the employee's

file. If you live in a state like Kentucky, your employees are "at-will." This means you can fire them easily, without a ton of red tape or bureaucracy. But if they later decide to bring an unemployment case against you, you'll need detailed records to defend yourself.

6. Be Their Boss, Not Their Friend – At the end of the day, you are the boss. Be an employee's boss… not their bestie. You can get to know them and be personable and friendly, but avoid gossiping at the bar on Saturday night, or having brunch on Sunday "just because." You can't hang out with them one night, and then address them the next day about a project issue or a missed deadline. As much as people say they can handle it, no one can truly flip that switch on and off. It will cause resentment and frustration in both directions.

7. Vetting Before the Hire – Do your research. Take the time to speak with references, schedule multiple interviews, and get candidates out of their comfort zone. The more you learn in advance, the less likely you'll end up with a bad hire. Some bad apples still slip through the cracks, but you can minimize this by discerning up front. We implemented a program for each new hire's first ninety days. It was basically an internship—we got to know them, and they got to know us. They worked on events with us, performed administrative work, and we saw how they worked with our team and our clients. At the end of the ninety-day period, we either offered them a full-time job, or we didn't. It saved us a ton of money and headache from hiring on the spot.

8. Go With Your Gut – Sometimes, you just "know." You get a feeling about an applicant, good or bad. Listen to that feeling, and take it into consideration.

9. Thinning the Herd – When shit employees slip through the cracks, eliminate the tension as quickly as possible. They cause issues and frustration in the office, they tarnish the culture—and that hurts your business. Don't let them walk all over you, and don't let them irritate the rockstars into leaving. As the saying goes, be "Slow to hire, and quick to fire." It took me ten years in business to learn this.

10. It Takes Time – Don't get frustrated with employees' levels of skill and competence. You will have people of different calibers. It takes time, work, and training (and re-training) people to get a team full of rockstars, but don't give up—you can do it. (You'll have to remind yourself of this often.)

Payroll and Taxes

This part is confusing and scary. You need to find an expert; you *cannot* do this on your own. You have to follow so many rules and pay so many taxes, and you'll find nothing scarier than having the IRS breathe down your neck.

Each city and state has taxes and laws for matching contributions. These are paid by employers, so you must count them as compensation for each new hire. Find a bookkeeper and CPA as soon as possible. Even if you're good with back-office work, you still need help and extra sets of eyes when filing taxes, processing payroll and staying above-board financially. *Do not* cross your fingers and hope you're correct. Early in my career, I tried to figure out taxes on my own. I didn't understand the complexity of state, versus city, versus federal taxes. And then you have payroll tax, versus sales tax, versus Social Security, versus some other tax I surely forgot to mention. It cost me tremendously. Let me tell you, you do *not* want to get a letter from the IRS. It's scarier than bankruptcy.

Fun Fact: When you are delinquent in your taxes, the IRS tacks on penalties and interest, and charges you *by the day*. It adds up quickly, and they won't call you to let you know you're behind. Then comes a big-ass bill in the mail that you can't afford to pay—because no one saves up for back taxes or penalties and interest. I naively thought, "Oh, I can surely dig myself out of this hole." I was wrong. For *five years*, I tried to dig myself out, costing me thousands of dollars. Seven years later, it finally ended. What a joke. (*If you prefer to save for taxes ahead of time, I recommend "Profit First" by author Mike Michalowicz.*)

Employees Will Never Work as Hard as You Do

This is frustrating, but true. I'm the first one in the office and the last to leave—and let's be honest, that's why I own my company, and my employees don't. Don't get frustrated that employees fail to match your levels of dedication and commitment. You need to find team players and hard workers and take care of them, but always remember: It's your name that gets signed on the dotted line, not theirs.

I had a true *rockstar* employee I "stole" from a manufacturing company where I oversaw their catering operations (externally) while she managed events (internally). She'd been looking for a change, and we worked *very* well together during her first year. LexEffect started to grow quickly, and I lost sight of the event management because I stayed focused on sales. She loved design work and was very talented at it, but she needed someone to oversee her work and keep her on track instead of doing it all on her own.

She started managing some of our other team members, and her then-boyfriend told me I should make her my partner. I usually laughed it off, but he was serious and frequently brought it up. I felt frustrated that she didn't put in *near* the hours or work I did. Her boyfriend constantly complained about how much she worked—which I pointed out when he nudged me for a partnership agreement. I gave her plenty of time off, often with no notice, when they'd have another argument over his wandering eye. But then he'd go right back to telling me that I needed to make her my business partner. She never came to me herself to tell me she wanted that! We could never become partners because we had an imbalance of "work" and commitment between us.

When you find employees who work hard, make it worth their effort. Offer incentives like extra vacation days, salary increases, bonus options, and revenue sharing to show gratitude for their hard work. Extra perks here and there make for a great working relationship. After years of learning what to avoid, I've honed how I manage rockstars. We moved to a remote work environment, which allowed our team to work from anywhere. They have a flexible work schedule, so they can adjust their working hours (within reason). We changed our benefits package and our work model for better work/life blend. Most of our employees and interns stay with us for years (like our current team), and even those who leave still do contract work for us from time to time.

More online:

Working For Their Paycheck

There's a difference between "revenue" employees and "task" employees. You need both, and depending on the industry you're in, you might need more of one than the other. Revenue employees are sales- or revenue-driven positions. They bring in money and increase profit for the company. (I would argue that *everyone* is a "sales" employee in a small or start-up company, but I digress).

On the other side of the coin, you have task employees. These people help take work off the plates of your sales employees, allowing them to do more selling. Bookkeepers, business managers, marketing directors, admins, and assistants fall under the category of task employees. They may not work directly with clients or customers, and they may not be responsible for sales, but their work allows others to focus on generating revenue. They help make the machine run efficiently.

While you need to care for your team, don't confuse "care" for *productivity*. At the end of the day, you still run a business and your employees still work for a paycheck. You need to make sure they're worth the expenses (salary, taxes, matching, benefits, etc). You should see your profit margin increase, either because a new employee brings in new revenue, or because they help your sales team bring in more.

We once had a new investor come on board, who asked me about our employees' productivity, experience, and work ethic. They wanted a list of all the business our employees brought in, divided by who brought in the business. One of them hadn't even covered half of her expenses and salary. She was a salesperson, and we paid out far more in expenses than she earned in revenue. The math didn't make sense. If scenarios like this are the norm, you won't stay in business long. She felt she contributed blood, sweat, and tears to the company—but we felt differently. Too many things slipped through the cracks, and she no longer earned her paycheck. We parted ways.

Being a Boss

Being a boss feels great when you create something new or guide your team members to success. But being a boss also sucks. It's hard, tiring, and sometimes ruthless. I thought life would get "even better" when I hired people. I hoped to be the CEO or president that goes to events, sips cocktails, and has a ton of free time because I direct traffic while the team does the heavy lifting. I was wrong. Hiring employees meant *more* work—especially for a small business like mine. I oversee payroll, bookkeeping, employee tasks, sales, client relations, marketing—the list goes on. (*Also, I have a hard time delegating.*)

Then there's the drama that comes with having a team of people working closely together. Unfortunately, as a small start-up, most of the "HR" work fell to me. I got to listen and talk about boyfriends and girlfriends, financial issues and personal issues, conflict between team members, late nights, school drama – *loads* of information that I didn't want (or need) to know. I'm not an overly emotional person anyway, so this much "sharing" gets exhausting for me, especially on top of my already-full plate.

If the team/company does well, you give them the credit.

If not, you take all the blame.

Employees are the best and worst parts of a growing company.

Being their age – If you're like me, you are most likely close in age with the people who work for you. This makes things awkward, especially when trying to be the boss. I've learned over the years that you must not be their friend. By "friend," I mean the person who goes out to the bar with them, gossips about their boyfriend/girlfriend, or hangs out on the weekend. You can't flip the switch between friend and manager day by day, despite your best efforts and intentions. Eventually, you may have to reprimand them, and people rarely take reprimands from their friends seriously.

Since you're close in age, you're at a disadvantage in being perceived as the boss, rather than as their peer or equal. I once managed a restaurant where most of the people I supervised were my friends. Prior to becoming their manager, I was one of their equals. I lived with some of them, and hung out with most of them. I once overheard my roommates talk about how they hated having me as their boss. They couldn't distinguish between the two roles and didn't want to take direction from me.

Managing people – Managing people is a juggling act. You are their boss, babysitter, project manager, therapist, teacher, coach, and so on. You have to wear each of these hats while keeping things on track, managing payroll, and attending to other business functions. Sometimes, even if you do it well, you still lose good employees when their lives change. Other times, despite your best efforts, you can't find the right employee. Every now and then, you get so tired that you don't want to deal with others' messes… but you have to.

Once you can hire a manager, do it. This person should become your chief of staff—your gatekeeper, so to speak.

Moving On – This may sound crass or heartless, but sometimes the best (and hardest) thing to do with employees is move on. This goes for both good employees and not-so-good employees. One of the toughest things for me is to let go and move on after investing time, money, and effort into training people. I want it to work, but as the leader of the organization, I have to serve the greater good. I look at the bigger picture; when it's time for someone to go, they must go.

I once had an amazing team member, Abby, who started with us as an intern. She interned for class credit, which led to part-time (and eventually full-time) work once she graduated from college. She was a hard worker—a go-getter and an amazing team member. She showed up early, stayed late, and was *always* ready to roll up her sleeves and get the job done.

During COVID, like most companies, we had to furlough our team to survive the pandemic. Abby was part of that team, and with style and grace, she furloughed with the rest of them. During that period, she decided she wanted to move to Denver and look for work there. I did *not* want Abby to leave, but I knew it was best for her. We had no idea when we would re-open or how long it would take us to recover. It wasn't fair for me to try and keep her. I helped connect her to employers I knew in Colorado and served as a glowing reference for her eventual job there.

Around the same time, we had a team member who worked on the venues side of our business. She came from a venue management background. On paper, she looked like a great fit. But for several reasons, she wasn't—and it began to show. Clients complained that they couldn't get quotes, email replies, or contact her by phone. It cost revenue we desperately needed. Some new clients went for weeks without responses. What a mess! After several reviews and conversations, we agreed that LexEffect wasn't the right fit for her. She found employment elsewhere, and that was the end of that.

Don't Hire Friends

Read this paragraph twice, because I'm serious. No matter how much you think you are an exception to the rule, <u>do *not* hire friends or family to work for you</u>. Nineteen times out of ten, it doesn't work. Your friends and family members cannot "pause" their relationship with you while in the office, no matter how much they try. They will take advantage of the relationship, seek favors and special treatment, other employees will resent them, and the end of the working relationship will ruin your personal one.

It took me four and a half hires to figure this out (despite several warnings that it was a bad idea).

One person claimed to "work" for me forty hours a week, but never showed up at the office. We had a flexible work schedule – Monday through Friday, 9am-5pm. But this person had a sales role, so his job, took him out of the office. As the leads and sales tapered off and he checked in less and less, I began to wonder how much "work" he truly did. I ran into his parents at a restaurant, and they mentioned how hard he was working, and how he wasn't around much anymore because of his workload and the hours spent at our office. They made it sound like I was over-working him, which came as a shock to me since I hadn't seen him for weeks.

Another friend/family employee told me they worked for me "as a favor," and that their role wasn't a real job. (*I'm sorry—I thought a salary, paycheck, and benefits meant you had a real job... my bad!*) Despite having a desk in our office, company-provided equipment and clothing, a bi-weekly paycheck, and a set schedule of office hours. they didn't consider it a "real job"—and said so regularly. I'm still not sure how that works.

Someone took advantage of my company to further their desire to hang out with musicians. We've produced some killer festivals and events, and that often includes musicians, comedians, authors, and performers. As our hospitality director, this person understood the artists and knew everything about them. But somehow, she thought that translated to "cracking open a beer during the event and kicking up your feet." (*It doesn't; instead, it means picking people up and dropping them off, restocking coolers and snacks, checking on hotels and shuttles and flights, and communicating with managers. She didn't seem to understand that... My fault, of course.*)

Someone else thought he was so advanced and experienced that he didn't need to show up to work or get anything done. He told me regularly about how his greatness and connections would "put us on the map."

I thought to myself, "Wonderful. Yes! Let's do that!" But what did it mean, you ask? It looked like dinners, events, tickets, and other expenses billed to the company for things that were irrelevant to our business—and no new or potential clients. You couldn't train this person. He "knew everything" already. And how do you tell your friend that they just aren't as good as they think they are?

I could go on forever about this. You might think, "Wow, Kaelyn—you need better friends!"

Maybe … but what I really needed were *better boundaries*. I needed to avoid hiring friends and family in the first place. All it took was one or two awkward interactions, and the whole relationship changed. Hear me out: it *never* works, you're asking for *trouble*, and you *won't* get the results you hope for.

There, I've said it.

INITIATIVE:
DEALING WITH CLIENTS

Chapter Extras

Customers are essential. You can't stay in business without them, right? But they're also the worst. I repeat… the *worst*.

Okay, that doesn't apply to *all* of them. Most actually turn out great, and some even become friends after the client relationship ends. But you'll always have difficult clients to deal with, and contrary to what you've heard, the customer is *not* always right.

Firing a Client

In all my years in this industry, I've only ever had to fire four clients, though I threatened it on two other occasions. It sucked every time I did it. Sometimes, you just don't see eye-to-eye with a client, no matter how hard you try. Other clients get unrealistic, or go way outside the scope of work without a willingness to adjust or pay extra. Once in a blue moon, you'll have to fire a client because of disrespectful behavior, breach of contract, or other unpleasant reasons.

Always be diplomatic in your decision. Firing a client has ramifications, and you shouldn't do it on a whim, or fueled by emotion. As much as I love a cuss word (or seven), dismissing a client should be well-worded and professional, just as you'd do with an employee. This goes on your "record" in the marketplace, and it will certainly get passed around to other people. You must choose your delivery (and reasoning) wisely. People talk, so do your best to avoid giving them reason to talk about you negatively.

Once, I fired a corporate client. We had plenty of time to think ahead and prepare for their event, which we appreciated. (*That's better than some of the "on-demand" miracles some clients prefer.*) We spent time and energy getting quotes for all their possible venues, including overnight accommodations, meeting space, reception space, transportation, and so forth. We ran a feasibility study and negotiated rates. We traveled for several meetings, site visits, and tours to make the final selection. We even negotiated extensions to the contract when they missed deadlines for signing and paying their deposit.

We'd schedule meetings to review updates, details, and next steps, but they never showed up on-time or prepared. At one point, they sent an email asking about an event detail, and they got an auto-reply saying I was out of town for one week. *One week*. This was on a Saturday, by the way, at 8AM, and I was due to return the following Friday. I already struggle with boundaries, especially with clients and work. I "found some time" to send what they needed while I was on the trip. *While on vacation*. On a Saturday.

Instead of acting respectfully, they followed up with several hateful emails complaining about my absence, whining about how much they "needed me," and lecturing about the inappropriateness of not telling them I was going out of town. Mind you, my trip was in February, and their event was at the end of May. We had no meetings scheduled while I was away. Whatever they could need or want could wait five business days. I assured them I would get them the information as soon as I got back, but their behavior worsened. I received an email demanding that I schedule a call with them that day, and they said I would "regret" not jumping to the occasion.

So we fired them.

Another time, a wedding client reached out to us to help plan and coordinate a wedding 1.25 years in advance (Yay!). We follow a process for onboarding new clients: a discovery call, a proposal, contract, and first payment received. All of these precede the actual work. This client asked for a lower-tiered package, but then demanded the moon—" Champagne taste on a beer budget," as we say. She wanted extra access to the venue without paying for it. She wanted a *seven-hour* reception (industry standard is 4-5 hours). She refused to pay overtime for the bar and catering staff, the band, or the bar fee. She wanted a videographer, but turned her nose up at the price and said, "It shouldn't cost this much." (*Don't get me started on this…*)

We met in-person on a Friday afternoon. I typically don't meet clients on Fridays, but they lived a couple of hours away from us, so I offered to accommodate their schedule. I told them I had to leave at 5PM to pick up my infant son from daycare (which closed at 5:30PM).

She expected me to spend more time with her, while refusing to pay my retainer fee. Then she demanded to meet with my designer *that night* to talk about invitations, for a wedding one and a half years away. Politely, I told her I would ask about the invitation designer's availability, but reminded her I couldn't control their schedule or availability, especially on a Friday night after 5PM with no notice. After a few weeks to think it through (and a few more instances of the same behavior), I called the client to let her know that we would be unable to help them with the wedding. I refunded their retainer immediately by mail. That breakup call was worse than any breakup I had in high school or college combined!

Another story: we worked on some continuing education events for a school system. Schools are bureaucracies that operate similarly to government clients. This client had big problems staying organized. The decision-makers never attended meetings, despite our efforts to schedule around their availability. They refused to provide a budget, and when we presented all of the pieces (based on their requests), they informed us we were way over budget—by hundreds of thousands of dollars. (*Isn't this fun?*)

The school system's event gathered over 8,000 people simultaneously across nine venues. Many vendors refused to work with them, based on negative past experiences and unpaid bills. Despite our best efforts and plans, one of their secretaries went over our head and changed details with vendors and venues—and purposely kept us in the dark about the changes. Another secretary—their in-house "event planner"—didn't show up to a single meeting. She left all of her responsibilities unattended. It was an absolute *cluster*. Two weeks before the event, I fired them. They called and pleaded with us to continue. They were now in a big hole without us, because we had all the knowledge and details worked out. Even though their team caused chaos—some of it intentionally—they still needed us.

I remained unwilling to risk my reputation on their shit show, and refused to proceed. After another round of pleading (and talking through it with the team), we realized we had a bigger risk to our reputation, no matter what we did. If we produced the event and it didn't go well, the client would blame us. But if we pulled out, they'd blame the chaos on our decision to quit. We went ahead and produced the event—and avoided that client from then on. (Their events are still a mess, by the way).

When clients push you to the point you consider firing them, take a good look at the situation and assess the potential consequences. In my mind, disrespecting my staff was a non-starter, and our vendors function like our extended team. When they get screwed, I get screwed—and I don't like others messing with my people. If you're going to fire a client, get ready to stand your ground. Be classy, be firm, but don't say anything you might regret. You never know when circumstances change, and you could end up working with them again! Keeping emotions out of it is the hardest part. I feel passionate about what I do and the company and reputation I've built. It's hard for me to avoid getting emotional when someone has the power to tarnish your reputation. Do not let emotions drive this bus.

Pricing

When working with new clients and customers, settle the question of value in your mind. Prices change, and expenses change. But what is the *value* of what you do? You have to make sure the job (or the client) is worth what you exchange to work with them. When I first started, I wanted to win every bid I submitted, and thought I failed when I didn't get a bid.

I realized I gave people prices too quickly just to get the bid in their hand and get a potential "Yes" without learning enough about their event. It would have been wiser to ask how many people they expected, what their needs were, where their pain-points were, and so forth. Instead, I had "base prices" I would shoot for, for events based on how

many days we needed for load-in and production. Whether you were a wedding for fifty people or a corporate event for five hundred, we charged the same amount for one-day events. More often than not, this resulted in an underpriced and over-budget plan, which ended up costing me on the back end.

You can't go back and change a proposal once you submit it, so make sure you price everything out and think about it dynamically. I've forfeited a lot of time and money over the years by not reviewing and revising my fees. Today, we use a process for quoting. Typically, inquiries come in by phone or email, so we start with the specific calendar date. How many times did I mess *that* up? Early in my career, I often submitted a proposal only to find out *after* sending the bid that we already had an event booked for their requested date!

If the date is available, we schedule a discovery call, usually by phone or video. I go through a list of questions, and work with the team to create a proposal based on… wait for it… *the actual details and needs of the event*! What a concept! If the client wants a one-day event for

More online:

10,000 people that requires a ton of work, we charge accordingly. And if they have a three-day event, but they only need us for registration, we adjust for that, too. We consider production days, load in/strike days, travel days, number of staff on site, number of areas covered, an estimate of planning and admin hours, and so on. Let's just say that today, my $500 event fee from 2013 wouldn't even cover our time spent closing the sale!

Once we send the proposal to the client, we schedule another call or virtual meeting to review and answer questions. Assuming they accept, we send the contract for signature and an invoice for first payment. Until we receive both contract and payment, we stay busy serving our existing clients. If you're good at something, never do it for free! I learned that the hard way. We produce fewer events today than ten years ago, but we earn more money. I now charge correctly for the service we provide, and I'm careful and meticulous with our process.

Personalities

I'll tell you my biggest weakness. I'm vocal, I wear my emotions on my sleeve, and I don't hide my thoughts or feelings well. Sometimes my personality doesn't mesh well with a client. I've learned to take personalities in stride, try to keep mine at bay, and keep the bigger picture at the forefront.

Despite my "directness" (and various other qualities), by nature I am a people pleaser, through and through. Early in my career, I wanted nothing more than to please everyone. If a client wanted a twenty-foot head table on a fifteen-foot wall, I'd say, "Sure, no problem!" If they wanted to bring their own alcohol even though it violated the venue's contract policies, I'd say, "We'll figure it out!" If you gave me a $40,000 budget but added six new vendor categories, doubled your guest count, and changed venues, I'd say, "We'll make it happen!"

More online:

Except that I couldn't make it happen. I couldn't figure it out, and I knew it. I got nervous when clients got direct with me or sounded upset. Even though they wanted something completely unrealistic, like the examples above, it scared me to death. Say the client originally approved $40,000. Then they acted shocked when the budget exceeded $75k after I worked out their over-the-top requests. I took it personally when they got upset. I wanted to make everything perfect; I thought it was my job. Yes, my job is to create a great experience, but I can only do so much—especially when I don't know the rules or expectations of the client.

If you pick a venue with a price tag that makes the rest of your event cost prohibitive, I can only do so much.

If you choose a caterer that did a really great job with sandwich trays for your office party, but they're completely unprepared for a corporate reception for 600 people ... I can only do so much.

If you disregard my advice during planning, and something goes haywire, I can only do so much.

I learned over the years that clients' shock and disappointments aren't personal—or at least, they shouldn't be. Today, I calmly and politely say, "Yes, the event has exceeded the original $40,000 budget because we changed locations and are now paying for a very expensive venue. We also increased our invitations by $5,500 from the original $500 estimation (going from digital to physical), and added two hundred additional people to the guest list. And because of our new venue, we have to pay for two shuttles, a fancy restroom trailer, signature cocktails, extra power, and labor overtime (among other things). None of this was accounted for in the original $40,000 budget. Is there an area you'd like me to try and cut to reduce the added expenses?" I am direct, firm, and polite, and I don't take it personally anymore. The client changed the scope ... not me.

I also learned that just because someone is short *with* me doesn't mean they are upset *at* me. Other factors cause them stress, and I just happen to be in their path. I have no need to overthink these interactions.

Adjusting to Personalities

You'll learn to adjust to all sorts of personalities. There's no one-size-fits-all model in business; you will upset somebody, somewhere. Some clients need their hands held, others don't. Some need to be praised, and some just want you to cut to the chase. Some need regular updates, and some want to be left alone. The hardest part of having a client is figuring out which type you're dealing with, and their expectations.

One of our biggest clients (as of writing) is a development company based in northern Kentucky. Our contact there does not micro-manage; she just wants the job done well. But when we review, she wants high-level overviews. She wants the key details, and she trusts us to make the small decisions. She hired us for this, after all.

On the opposite side of the coin, we have a government client we produce a conference for every year. They operate by committee, which means we have a harder time getting approvals and final answers. No one on their side ever really takes the "lead," which means we have to stay on top of them, over-communicate, check-in often, and send lots of recap emails to ensure everyone actually stays on the same page.

We've learned through experience to adjust to each client. We even ask in the beginning of working with a new client how we can best communicate with them. Do they prefer our project management portal? Or do they prefer email communication?

More online:

Clients Who Overstep

Some clients overstep their roles, boundaries, and project scopes. You have to keep that in check. I used to get defensive, but I've learned to pick my battles. If it's something minor in the grand scheme, then let them "win" and move on. But if they cross into an area where you cannot allow them to overstep, politely work your way through the subject.

We once had a client that wanted to micromanage every detail of their event, from menu items to colors, to stage skirting, to the power cables used by the audio visual team. Some of it didn't really matter in the grand scheme. They wanted a different menu; we didn't think it was the best menu for the event, but okay—we went with fried chicken in June… outdoors.

Another client wanted to change the event setup. The changes would cause chaos and congestion, as well as block emergency exits – a major risk in the event of emergency. We refused to change the format—it violated fire code, and it risked the safety of those at the event. I declined to be liable for that, so the answer was "No." Sometimes, clients just need reminders that you know what you're doing and they can trust you.

Clients Aren't You

At the end of the day, you're the expert with the passion. Your clients may claim they understand, and they may want to—but they don't. You must train and coach them. You can't expect them to know how to do something or share your passion. While you perform, you must spend time training, coaching, and teaching your clients the ins and outs of what you do for them. Above all else, keep hold of your passion no matter how hard it gets. If you lose your passion, your clients will lose faith in you.

One time, I produced a client's fundraising event that should have been a smashing success. Those involved had clear roles from the beginning, but like so many non-profit committees, they had too many cooks in the kitchen and no food to cook with. The event itself went off with little-to-no hiccups. However, it only sold 150 tickets (of 2000 needed) and lost money.

I didn't listen to my gut when it told me to halt several issues happening within the planning committee. They were booking unpopular bands based on recommendations from a friend they considered an "expert." The event date they chose was Election Day 2016, the day Donald Trump became president-elect. It was a *bad* day to host a fundraiser.

After the event ended, I met with one of the committee members. We had differing opinions of who should do what. He began spreading his distaste for us around the community and stirring up rumors. He even threatened to sue us for "non-performance" and damages. There were many aspects I should have handled differently, but in the final analysis, we did our job and exceeded our contract. When I met with the committee member, he told me he wanted me to "fall on my sword" and take the blame for the failure of the event. He hoped I would come to their next board meeting and say, "I am the expert; this was my fault, and I will make it right."

But it was *not* my fault, and I refused to take all of the blame. We learned several hard lessons we'll never forget, and we will never work with them again.

I made several mistakes with this client. Our contract had clear terms about our tasks, but no clear list of what we should not do. Don't assume that everyone knows; put it in print. I failed to give them clear direction on what they should do or what materials they needed. (*I assumed they knew.*) I saw early signs that the "committee" wasn't fulfilling their end of the deal. I treaded on this lightly; in hindsight, I should have immediately called it out. This is the "training and coaching" part of client success every business owner must learn.

INNOVATION:
WHITE NOISE

10 | **BAD DEALS**
BAD IDEAS
"GREAT" OPPORTUNITIES
COMPETITION
VENDORS
CONTRACTS
MISTAKES AND **MOVING ON**

Chapter Extras

When you start a business, you quickly encounter "white noise" distractions. They consume your time, money, and patience. Don't let this happen to you.

Bad Deals

One form of white noise is *deals and opportunities*. You'll come across a lot of deals out there; some seem great, and some truly are. But you'll find just as many bad ones. Don't get involved in them. Do research, crunch the numbers, and spend time thinking about each one. As I've said, I've agreed to some really bad deals in the past, and I'm still paying the consequences for some of them.

Remember my bad musical festival deal? The concert itself always went well, but one year, we came up short financially. I took on two business partners who bought 25% each of the company, while I retained 50 percent. I got so involved trying to solve my cash-flow issue that I failed to do my due diligence on these partners or the deal they offered.

When I made the initial deal, I was too preoccupied and worried about stepping on toes by asking questions. I was trying to solve a problem, quickly and painlessly. It ended up being the worst three years of my life. Is your company worth a bad deal? Be careful how you answer, because one bad deal is all it takes to bring your business crashing down. And think about more than just money; bad deals can also destroy your reputation, force you to hire bad employees, expose you to lawsuits, and get you stuck in contracts you can't nullify.

More online:

Bad Ideas

But never mind damage from doing bad deals with other people; you'll come up with plenty of bad ones on your own! I have concepts or ideas I've tried that failed miserably. Sometimes a concept seems "great" in theory, but when you put it on paper, it makes a lot less sense. If it passes the paper test, sometimes it still collapses in the planning phase. And sometimes it gets through planning and all the way to production… but the marketplace yawns. Them's the breaks.

You need people and methods to vet your ideas. If concepts make it past the initial phase and you take action, you also need to examine the results and determine what went wrong, minimize damage, and make adjustments to move forward. I highly recommend a "phased" approach at pursuing your ideas. Set deadlines or certain milestones. If you don't hit the milestone, pivot or stop. When we organize events, we set milestones based on financial benchmarks, like ticket sales and sponsorships. If we don't hit those numbers by a certain date, we know ahead of time that an event is unlikely to be profitable. We've even developed metrics to decide at that point whether we cancel, pivot, or proceed. You can turn bad ideas into great assets if you manage the process well.

"Great" Opportunities

As soon as I opened, I got flooded with "great opportunities" to partner with others, start additional companies, or bring partners on for my business. You have to take these for what they are: opportunities. One group of people approached me about partnering on a New Year's Eve party. We'd already hosted our own lucrative event, but it cost a significant amount to produce. Whenever possible, I think it benefits you to have partners. You might forfeit some winnings, but you take on less risk. So we decided to partner with this group—and that was the first, last, and only time we felt good about the agreement.

I didn't yet realize the importance of good contracts because I hadn't fallen prey to bad ones yet! We had a handshake agreement, and from that moment, everything changed. They didn't hold to a single word of their agreement. They stole liquor, overcharged guests, and failed to provide the food, rentals, or staff they had committed to. The guests liked the event, but we spent the entire night scrambling to fix issues from the moment the doors opened.

Just like ideas or deals, you need to think opportunities through. Explore and examine them thoroughly. Don't jump on something quickly just because someone approaches you about it. Ask yourself: Do I have enough time to invest in this opportunity? Do I have the money? How will it affect my current company? Does it present a conflict of interest? What will the split be? Could I do this on my own just as easily?

In the first 3-5 years of business, I would steer clear of these opportunities unless they line up with current business practices (and don't pose conflicts). Find reasons to avoid them, and put them on the back burner until you are more stable.

Competition

If you have a growing business, you'll eventually attract competitors —folks trying to mimic or copy what you do. It's flattering, but beware! Don't spend too much time worrying about other people's actions and plans. If you already do a good job, just keep doing it. People will notice. Others will try and copy you, and that's fine—let them. They will either succeed and capture their own share of the market, or they'll fail and move on.

Even so, don't show competitors all of your cards. I notoriously talk, and too damn much. Have you ever heard the saying "Loose lips sink ships"? Talking too much about your plans invites people to come along and beat you to the punch. One year, an event planner moved into the Lexington area from a bigger city. Her husband was friends with the guy I dated at the time, who asked me to meet with her as a favor since she didn't know anyone in town. I talked about the wedding industry, the market, corporate events, and so forth.

We continued to run into each other, and I noticed how she "popped up" at all the same events and groups as I did. She followed the same plan, even using some of the same contract language (verbatim). She started opening business ventures identical to mine. I thought I was being friendly and generous, but really I just handed her my playbook.

Keep your cards close to the chest, and don't talk too much with competitors. Don't be surprised if someone offers to "help" you, only to turn around and poach your ideas. Don't tell people what you're going to do, just go do it – and let them react to it.

More online:

Vendors

Vendors can be your greatest asset, or biggest headache. Sometimes both.

I previously mentioned a florist in my market who treated me well early in my business. I didn't know anything about flowers. I could barely keep a bouquet alive, and I certainly didn't know about floral design or arrangements. She helped my business, supported me, recommended me—and to this day, I work with her for 90% of our events. We have a mutual agreement: I take care of her, and she takes care of me. (*We're both direct, blunt people who understand each other well... so that helps.*) When my business fell into trouble, she told me to keep selling her flowers and she'd let me pay it off over longer periods of time. She's also saved my butt a time or two when a client made a last-minute request, or I screwed something up.

Elsewhere, I tried an exclusive agreement with a local rental company that offered a preferred rate for my clients. But their managing director left to join another company, they went through some big turnover with staff, and things went downhill from there. The new staff treated us rudely, and one of their salespeople hated me (*still* unsure why). At times they wouldn't rent to us, and wouldn't give us a reason. They still talk negatively about us to other vendors. We moved to another rental company and built a lasting partnership there.

Vendors who recommend you will serve as the backbone of your business. Without trustworthy vendors, your job gets ten times harder. My industry is a small community, which implies plenty of gossip and trash talk. Competitors don't necessarily support one another, cliques form, and it can get ruthless. To avoid this, stay above and out of the fray. Be respectful, avoid "he said, she said," and be the kind of person you would want to work with. Reject the middle school mindset; you gain nothing by sinking to that level. Instead, maintain good vendor relationships that make your company run smoothly.

Contracts

In the beginning, I had a habit of negotiating poor contracts, or not having them at all. Our first full-service client was an old music venue. We worked with the owners from start to finish. We created the brand, logo, name, and aesthetic. We built their operations, sales structure, social media accounts, and marketing plan. Once the space opened, we managed the venue for public and private events. But we had a poorly-written contract that gave the client full control while we did all the work. We were unprotected.

All the revenue went to the client to "hold." They commingled it with other money, which meant we had to request payment each month for our fees, supplies, etc. We fought a constant battle to get paid, as well as to get updates from the client when checks had arrived. It added a lot of stress and extra work.

Aside from private events, the goal was to have public, ticketed events. The clients loved country music, but turned up their noses at any other genre we tried to put in the space. Although Lexington is a big market for country, there were plenty of opportunities from other genres, too. But did those clients listen or consider alternatives? Nope! Instead, they pushed us to host shows that we knew would lose money. When the shows didn't produce, they'd get mad and blame us. After a while, they stopped paying our fees and their marketing bills. They even stopped buying toilet paper for the venue! Eventually, they said they were finished working with us… and I hired a new attorney.

Unfortunately, the agreement we drafted had no language about termination, or anything about past due fees, expenses, and revenue shares. We tried to meet several times with their attorney and each time, they blew us off. Our attorney eventually advised us to move on and chalk this up as a lesson. (*How many "lessons" do you think I had to learn before I became "successful"?*)

Those clients still owe me a lot of money, and I know I'll never see a penny of it. I was okay at negotiating, and I had some idea of what I was doing. But I failed to give the contracts the time and attention they needed. Make sure you get well-written contracts and understand what they say. In the beginning, we had far too many circumstances where someone agreed to something and failed to follow through. I didn't have proper contracts in place, nor did I think through the ones I had. The company grew, and I mishandled bigger contracts with the same issue: fail-safe provisions for when clients failed to meet their end of the bargain. You have to make sure the contracts cover you and that every area gets written out.

Your contracts must be complete, including terms, policies, and clear statements of what you will and won't do. Don't assume someone knows, or they're on the same page as you. Write it out, discuss it, and sign off on it. Even then, you may still have to defend it in court. In the event industry, we watch closely for "venue" clauses—the city, county or state where the case goes to court in case of a dispute. Check for language about arbitration, court, or disagreements—and who gets held responsible for those fees. If you are based in Kentucky and the contract follows the laws of Delaware, you might get in trouble later if any legal issues arise.

With MoonTower Music Festival, I missed the "venue" clause in one of the contracts. It was set for California. This meant that the plaintiffs sued me in California. So I had to hire a California attorney to represent my Kentucky attorney, who in turn represented me. That meant two hourly rates for every call or meeting, plus many other expenses. I'll never make that mistake again.

Mistakes and Moving On

Even with these guidelines, I still make mistakes. After all the lessons about contracts, venue clauses, payment terms, business partners, and operating agreements—I still screw up. One time, I got an opportunity to own and operate a high-profile venue: the original courthouse in Lexington, Kentucky. The 100+ year-old building sat vacant and run-down for years. A group of people and organizations developed a plan to raise funds to rehab the courthouse and give it new life. I planned to lease the top floor and turn it into an event space. It took off!

When I embarked on this journey, I felt determined to avoid the mistakes I made before with contracts. This was the largest project I'd had up to that point, and I'd guaranteed a *lot* of money. I brought in my attorney from the start. I had advisors help guide me, and I had some folks on the inside steering me in the right direction. The project manager tried to pull a few things over my head (they thought I wasn't paying attention or didn't know any better... but the joke was on them).

This time, I did everything right—the way I learned to do it from all the hard lessons I experienced. But from the day we opened our doors until the day I sold the business, the building (and the property managers) were a disaster. All of the tenants were unhappy, and unfortunately, I couldn't do anything about it. It didn't matter that I "followed the rules"

and paid attention and took all the precautions and necessary steps; there were still issues beyond my control that served to sabotage the effort.

The way you bounce back from mistakes defines you. Don't let them consume you, don't dwell on them, and don't let them stop you from kicking ass the next day. Pull yourself up by your bootstraps, and keep going.

More online:

INNOVATION:
FRIENDS & FAMILY

11 | **THEY DON'T UNDERSTAND**
MONEY AND **FREE TIME**
AS A SUPPORT SYSTEM
KEEPING PERSPECTIVE
STAY IN TOUCH

Chapter Extras

Friends and family are your support system. You work hard for them. They build you up. But they can just as easily bring you down. In this chapter, we'll look at some of the ins-and-outs of business when it comes to friends and family.

They Don't Understand

I don't care how much your friends and family support you, how involved they are in the process—they will never understand what it's like to start, run, and own a company. My dad, supportive as he is, still doesn't understand what I do. To this day, he scratches his head when I talk about events and event management, and he wonders how I make a full-time living "planning parties."

When I graduated college, all my friends applied for jobs. They had salaries, benefits, and vacation days. I had none of those. I got excited about growing revenues to the point I could (one day) draw a paycheck. I was different, and they didn't understand. I missed birthdays, holidays, celebrations, and trips. Who would sign up for all this work? And why miss so many opportunities? Why take on the stress, the juggling act, or the happy face you paint on when you really want to crawl under a rock and die?

For the most part, your friends and family "clock in, and clock out." They have lives, vacation days, holiday comp time, and maybe a group text about "hardly working Fridays." They won't understand what you go through, so find someone else to lean on when you need to talk or vent about business ownership. Let friends and family be who they are; they don't need to be your therapists as well.

Money and Free Time

The worst misconception people have about new business owners is that we already have money. Nope. Wrong! We are broke as shit. We put all our money into the business, or drain our savings to avoid taking a paycheck in the beginning. Any way you slice it, no start-up rolls in dough from the beginning. So get over the notion that starting your own business means you set your own pay. Set your pay to $0, and you'll be right on the money. (*See what I did there?*)

When you start a small business, the first two things you surrender are time and money. Go back to the exercise on page 4, and do it again.

More online:

As a Support System

You need a support system, but different from the one we discussed in Chapter Six. This system is comprised of people *not* involved in your business. I love including my friends and family in this. I go on spring break with a group of 46 people. *Forty-six* kids and adults—all in one house. It's chaotic—and great. Several of the adults are teachers, some are business owners, one is in development, one is an engineer, and two are nurses. I'm not sure what everyone does on a day-to-day basis in real life. Nor do they know about me, for that matter.

We don't come to talk about work (although sometimes it organically comes up in conversation). We spend the week laughing, playing games, and sitting on the beach. There are a few late night dance parties, and a very intense washers tournament throughout the trip. We have a *lot* of fun, and occasionally if I'm up in my room, I'll check in on something business related without saying a word to anyone else. Spending time with friends and family is a great way to take a break from work. Make sure to stay present in the moment. These times don't come around every day, so make the most of them.

More online:

Keeping Perspective

They may not say it, but friends and family admire what you do. They see the dedication, courage, and hard work. They cheer for you, even if they don't know how to say it. Sometimes they look at you in awe; what you do takes guts, and few of them have the same resolve to try it themselves. Don't lose sight of the "story" your life tells to others.

Be sure to have "anchors" to help you keep things in perspective. When my mother passed, I faced a hard stop from reality, a stark reminder that nothing is guaranteed and that emails can wait. When she passed, my community showed up in force. They jumped in to help with work, took care of our son, sent meals, and came and sat with me as I grieved. They did all they could to anchor me.

Stay in Touch

There will be seasons where you cannot spend as much time with friends and family as you want. They diminish your connection with people, and force you to miss important events and moments. Don't lose touch with them completely. Send something as simple as a text, a card, or a call—even a brief message lets folks know you still exist and remember them. Busy seasons don't last forever, and eventually you'll hire staff, create systems and processes, and stop working eight days a week, twenty-five hours a day. Until then, stay connected to the people who matter most.

On the other hand, don't overdo it, either. In the time you spend with your family and friends, the last thing to do is push your business on them. If they ask, you can certainly update them on the happenings of your business, but keep it short and sweet. They want to be supportive, but remember—they don't understand. Don't vent about business, or push products or services unless they ask. If you push too much, you becomes a nuisance, and folks won't want you around.

The first few years of my business, I'd see friends occasionally at the holidays. They'd ask the generic, "What have you been up to?" I'd take the opportunity to talk a mile a minute, telling them about all the "cool" things I'd done, how great things were going, and how successful I was. I wanted to prove to them that things had turned out just fine, despite the choices I made. No one asked me that question twice! I quickly learned to say, "Things are great!" and then ask them questions about *their* lives. If they wanted to talk further, they asked.

List Family & Friend Priorities Here
Trips, dinners, game nights, events, and so on...

131

INNOVATION:
THE ALTERNATIVE

Chapter Extras

There's always the alternative.

Work For Someone Else

You could go back to a desk job, clocking in and out, and working for someone else. But let's be serious—if you got this far, you aren't suited for a 9-5 job sitting at a desk. And you are probably not a great hire, because you're vocal and push limits, which doesn't lend itself well to a desk job.

But you can always go back to that job instead of building a business. After all, you now have a top-notch resume. You've built a business, managed a team, run finances, done the marketing, and all at the same time. You work well under pressure, manage your time well, and since you've hired other people, you know exactly what an interviewer looks for in a candidate.

As you know, I've done that too. I was tired of being in charge, doing everything and being "on call." Post-COVID, I was tired of the entire industry. We had a small team and produced over two hundred events a year between the two companies. We were making *great* money, but it no longer felt worthwhile. My son was growing up, I'd committed to a serious relationship, and I realized life was slipping away again. I missed a lot of important things.

So I sold the venue business, closed my event management company, and went to work for someone else. I found a company similar to mine based in California, applied for and got a job as an event producer. It was the same work I did in my own company, but I made a lot less money and far fewer decisions. I lasted five months there before they announced a mandatory, company-wide furlough with less than a month's notice.

Desk Jobs

The end of my job in California brought something else to mind: I don't like to depend on others for my income or schedule. Since we're talking about desk jobs, let me ask: Do you *really* want to work for someone else? Do you want to go back to someone else's deadlines and punch a clock? Do you want the stress of inter-office drama, a boss's bad moods, or interns who don't do anything?

More online:

You'll search far and wide for a desk job where you make your own decisions and work for a greater goal or bigger picture. It's hard to do on someone else's behalf. I loved my boss at that California company. We "clicked." I appreciated and respected her, and we worked well together. I felt disappointed I hadn't met her years ago; we could have made great business partners.

However, during my short time with that company, I felt the pressure of working for someone else. While they boasted about "flexible work hours," their culture didn't match the employee handbook. On several occasions, they asked me to get a babysitter so I could attend unnecessary internal meetings at night. They bragged you could "work from anywhere," but I got flack for working from a hotel in Florida the day before my approved vacation time (which was also the day before Thanksgiving). I experienced micromanaging and overstepping, and I received inconsistent direction. I sensed a *lot* of tension within the company, and it trickled down to everything else. I saw constant reminders that desk jobs didn't fit me.

I work hard—more hours per week than most people. But as an owner, I *decide* if I need to take a longer break for my mental health. If I want to, I *decide* to take a Friday off and shoot down to the lake or work from our cabin in Northern Michigan for two weeks. Do you notice how I used the word "decide"? It's my call.

Exhilaration

I'm driven by making sales, hitting goals, breaking barriers, and blowing expectations out of the water. I thrive on setting targets, exceeding them, and kicking ass at every milestone along the way. Starting a business has downsides, but I have more days where I think about our accomplishments with admiration for what got us here. I remember all the bad contracts, silly employee issues, money struggles, and the attempts to get ahead … only to fall behind once again. These get surpassed by thinking about the successful company I've built, considering its potential, and working towards the next level. I've had a long journey, and I'll be damned if I give up now.

My dad always said, "One day you'll look back at this and laugh." I used to get *so* annoyed by that comment, because he usually said it during moments when I didn't feel like laughing, and couldn't see beyond the present. But now, I look back at the bankruptcy, cash flow, back taxes… and he was right. I do laugh. (*But don't tell him I said*

More online:

that.) I laugh because I know that I am who I am today because of those experiences. They didn't kill me; I survived and became even better.

Create Your Own Way

You chart your course, do it your way, and call the shots. You walk this path by design. You can read and follow this guide and ten others like it, but you'll make your own mistakes and luck. You get to look back one day and see your accomplishments. Only you know the struggles you face and how you overcome them, and only you can decide what's next.

If You Can Make It Work

*I*f you make it past one year, as few companies do, and then you make it past years 3-5 and thrive, your efforts and sacrifices will be worth it. The stress, sleeplessness, loss of friends and money – all of it. Starting a business is a long shot and a bigger challenge than you can imagine, but if you can make it work, it will be worth it. SO worth it.

If You Can't, It Will Still Be Worth It

Even if it doesn't work, it's still worthwhile. You try, you give your all, and risk bravely. You do more than most people can say—and learn many valuable lessons that stay with you. Every year, I speak on a panel for students at the College of Communications at the University of Kentucky. They ask questions about internships, volunteering, jobs, and the hiring process. I always tell them that each job, task, and opportunity along the way are stepping stones to the next. It's going to get you to the next place, which gets you closer to the end goal. It might be part of that path, or the end result itself—who knows? But if you show the courage to try, you gain wisdom and experience, which are of even greater value.

It Doesn't Happen Overnight

*Y*ou must pass milestones on your road to success. The first six chapters of this book cover my *first* year of business, which was a huge milestone. If you make it through the first year, you have a fighting chance. In years 2-5, I fought like hell—bootstrapped, hustled, and busted my ass to make things work. Even then, it still had a big

More online:

chance of failure. It takes time – how much time it will take for you I can't say. But one day, *you* will know. At the time of writing I am in my 20th year in the event industry, and 11th as a business owner.

Make It a Five-Year Plan

Start your business with a five-year plan. It may take longer than five, but anything worth doing is worth more than one year of effort. Aa five-year plan projects revenues, growth plans, and hiring on a long-term basis. Be sure to update and adjust the plan, and assume from the beginning that it will take at least that long to work through these details. If you aren't a "big picture" type of person, find someone who can help you. Buckle up, and hold on tight, you have a bumpy ride ahead.

List Your Five Year Goals Here

CONCLUSION

So there you have it. You've made it this far, and you're still here. How do you feel? Let's revisit the activity you completed at the beginning of this book.

Circle the items below that matter to you the most.
Choose the ones you would <u>refuse</u> to give up to start your small business.
Total your score, one point for each item. We will revisit this later at the end of the manual.

10 Family
9 Friends
8 Money
7 Nights and weekends off
6 House, car, other property
5 Vacations
4 Steady pay checks
3 Events with your friends
2 Freedom
1 Making your own schedule

Total Score: _____

Are your numbers the same? Do you still want to launch, or continue to grow your business? If you've answered yes - where do you go from here?

The answer is, "This is just the beginning." Whether you're launching a business or already three to five years in, this is just the start. You and your business will ebb and flow as the months pass. I encourage you to sit with the work you've done (hopefully you did it), and let it soak in. Think deeply through what next steps look like for you. And then? Well, maybe you'll start over. Again and again. Not just with your business (although, maybe with new businesses), but also with yourself.

Use the worksheets to "check in" on your progress. Are you following your business plan? Are your finances in check? Are you keeping good boundaries and achieving your goals? You can't just do the exercise once and expect your life to change. It takes over 60 days to form a new habit. And work like this will take a lot longer. Continue to check in on yourself and your progress and adjust as needed.

Do you want more content? Then join our mailing list for monthly emails packed with tips, tricks, inspiration, and funny (horror) stories from my business journey. You can join via my website.

Still need more? I invite you to tune in to **Big Ideas, Small Business**, a podcast exploring the good, the bad, and the ugly of owning, operating, launching, and running a small business. You can link directly to this on my website, or you can find it anywhere you listen to your favorite podcasts.

Still need MORE?! Let's connect! I'm happy to speak to your organization, business, at an event, or lead a workshop. We also host workshops. So if you want to connect to other business owners and like-minded individuals, then come join us for a deep-dive into business excellence!

Keep going. You can do this. You are worth it and you matter. If you work hard enough, you can do anything you put your mind to. You will make a difference, and you will crush it.

And it will be SO worth it.

More online:

www.ingramcontent.com/pod-product-compliance
Lightning Source LLC
Chambersburg PA
CBHW040819120626

46551CB00005B/605